W9-AFG-065

Praise for *Why Religion?*

NATIONAL BESTSELLER

NEW YORK TIMES EDITORS' CHOICE

"In clear, unsparing prose, Pagels enmeshes personal mourning, scholarly rigor, and one of the smartest modern testaments to the consolations as well as the inadequacies of spirituality. A small revolution in memoir to match the one she led in theology decades ago."
—*New York* magazine

"A wide-ranging work of cultural reflection and a brisk tour of the most exciting religion scholarship over the past 40 years.... Pagels is as fearless as she is candid."
—*Washington Post*

"Pagels ... looks back on a rich life of learning, writing, loving, seeking truth and, inevitably, suffering.... Achingly beautiful.... Readers of all faiths and none can learn from her brilliance and courage."
—*Dallas Morning News*

"A story of depth and compassion.... Her memoir is anguished, poignant and contains unexpected moments of grace. It reads, in many ways, like a gnostic text of its own filled with hidden wisdom that is slowly revealed."
—*Post and Courier* (Charleston)

"Extraordinary—testimony to the depths of human despair and the elastic breadth of resilience. Facing the indescribable loss of two people closest to her, [Pagels] addresses the tangled tasks of dealing with guilt and its sibling anger, while surviving a journey through unimaginable pain.... This book, both radiant and opaque, deserves more than one reading."
—*Washington Times*

"Beautiful. . . . Pagels treats readers to the examined life behind her intellectual feats with extreme grace and depth. This luminous memoir strips religion to its elementary particles: love, suffering, and mystery." —*Publishers Weekly* (starred review)

"Pagels' powerful memoir-cum-meditation on religion reveals the power of religious rhetoric and defines its place in the world today." —*Paste* magazine

"A quiet meditation on the meaning of human mortality." —*Christian Science Monitor*

"One need not know the complexity of an ancient Greek verb to ponder her message or to enjoy this book." —*Star-Ledger* (Newark)

"Pagels has always been fiercely invested in the life of the mind, as well as in the lasting effects of the biblical stories that, whether or not we personally believe in them, have shaped the way we live and how we allow ourselves to think and behave. *Why Religion?* comes at a time when society is actively questioning basic assumptions about gender and power that were established in the Old Testament." —*Santa Fe New Mexican*

"You don't have to be religious yourself to enjoy her thought-provoking work." —Bustle

"Engaging both head and heart . . . this brilliant book . . . stimulates intellectual curiosity and thought while giving equal weight to Pagels's emotional life." —*Booklist* (starred review)

"Both fascinating and heart-wrenching, Pagels's highly personal account presents behind-the-scenes glimpses into the inner workings of a brilliant scholar's mind." —*Library Journal*

"A raw and often moving autobiography. . . . The story of her grief . . . will touch all. A meaningful tale of pain and hope on the edges of faith." —*Kirkus Reviews*

"[A] lucid, inspiring personal testimony."

—National Book Review, "5 Hot Books"

"Pagels unpacks the relevance of religion in the twenty-first century—how religious traditions continue to shape the way we understand ourselves and the world and provide a framework for facing our most painful losses." —*Lion's Roar*

"In this compelling, honest, and learned memoir, Elaine Pagels, who has arguably done more than any other scholar of her time to shed light on the complex origins of Christianity for popular audiences, takes us inside her own life in a stirring and illuminating effort to explain religion's enduring appeal. This is a powerful book about the most powerful of forces."

—Jon Meacham, author of *The Soul of America*

"With characteristic intelligence and wisdom, Elaine Pagels lays bare her own life-shattering losses, offering up the possibility that suffering might afford each of us membership in a profoundly connected human—and cosmic—community. *Why Religion?* is a revelation and an immense consolation."

—Tracy K. Smith, Poet Laureate of the United States

"The brilliant, tender, and irredeemably wise Elaine Pagels has not only produced here one of the twenty-first century's essential memoirs, she has also written, with characteristic incisiveness and poetic skill, about the mystery of grace—as symbol and fact. *Why Religion?* feeds the soul as it opens the mind. Reading it is like listening to Aretha Franklin and James Cleveland sing "Precious Lord": pure astonishment." —Hilton Als, author of *White Girls*

"Elaine Pagels has written an extraordinary memoir of loss, spiritual struggle, illumination, and insight—emotionally heartrending, intellectually exciting, a model of what a memoir should be. The reader will feel that she has been taken on a spiritual quest into unforeseen regions, with astonishing revelations and a promise of more to come." —Joyce Carol Oates

"Pagels has done it again, but more personally. The scholar's tale of loving, grieving, enduring, and searching will grab readers at the outset and never let them go. A memorable story unforgettably told."
—Madeleine Albright, author of *Fascism: A Warning*

"This is a magnificent, searing, soul-affirming memoir in which Elaine Pagels shines the bright light of her brilliant mind on the most essential of human dilemmas: How do we go on in the face of immeasurable loss? How do we wrest meaning from whatever life hands us? I came away from this book transformed, grateful, and feeling less solitary in the chaos, the beauty, the terror of this world."
—Dani Shapiro

"Elaine Pagels's study of new gospels and revelations challenged our understanding of ancient Christianity. In this mesmerizing memoir, we see how she was also grappling with devastating loss and struggling within to find 'the light that never fails,' even in deepest anger and guilt, grief and desolation. A must-read."
—Karen L. King, Hollis Professor of Divinity, Harvard University

Why Religion?

ALSO BY ELAINE PAGELS

The Johannine Gospel in Gnostic Exegesis:
Heracleon's Commentary on John

The Gnostic Paul:
Gnostic Exegesis of the Pauline Letters

The Gnostic Gospels

Adam, Eve, and the Serpent:
Sex and Politics in Early Christianity

The Origin of Satan:
How Christians Demonized Jews, Pagans, and Heretics

Beyond Belief:
The Secret Gospel of Thomas

Reading Judas:
The Gospel of Judas and the Shaping of
Christianity (with Karen L. King)

Revelations:
Visions, Prophecy, and Politics in the Book of Revelation

Why Religion?

A PERSONAL STORY

ELAINE PAGELS

ecco

An Imprint of HarperCollins*Publishers*

HarperCollins books may be purchased for educational, business,
or sales promotional use. For information, please email the Special
Markets Department at SPsales@harpercollins.com.

A hardcover edition of this book was published in 2018 by Ecco, an
imprint of HarperCollins Publishers.

FIRST ECCO PAPERBACK EDITION PUBLISHED 2020.

Designed by Suet Yee Chong
Photographs courtesy of the author

Library of Congress Cataloging-in-Publication Data has been applied for.

ISBN 978-0-06-236854-6

20 21 22 23 24   LSC   10 9 8 7 6 5 4 3 2 1

To Sarah and David
with love

CONTENTS

Note on Translations

Translations from the *Gospel of Thomas* are by Marvin Meyer and Elaine Pagels, published as an appendix in *Beyond Belief: The Secret Gospel of Thomas* (New York: Random House, 2003).

Other translations from the Nag Hammadi Library follow the format in *The Nag Hammadi Library*, edited by James M. Robinson (Leiden, The Netherlands: Brill Press, 1978; republished in paperback in New York by HarperCollins, 1990).

INTRODUCTION

"And what do you do?" asked a man at the crowded reception at the New York Academy of Sciences, where my husband, Heinz, a theoretical physicist, was the director. "Write—about the history of religion." Startled, he backed away, as if afraid I might clamp a hand on his shoulder and say, "Brother, are you saved?" Hearing this, someone else asked, *"Why religion?* Why do *that*? Are you religious?" *Yes, incorrigibly*—although I grew up among people who regarded religion as obsolete as an outgrown bicycle stashed in a back closet.

Some people ask "What do you believe?" as if looking for someone to tell them what *they* should believe, or *not* believe—questions I can't answer, since I'm not a theologian who talks about God. Instead, I'm a historian who talks about human beings and the cultures we create. Other people, though, are asking what motivates the work: "Is this just an intellectual exercise for you, or are you engaged—and, if so, how?"

Responding to that question, I started with one of my own: *Why is religion still around in the twenty-first century?* Throughout the seven years of writing this book, I've been grateful to talk with anthropologists, political scientists, sociologists, neurologists, and psychiatrists, as well as artists, poets, and countless other people. Yet while I've woven many of those conversations into this book, the writing became intensely personal, showing how exploring the history of religion connects with experiences in my own life.

More than twenty-five years ago, when the death of our young child, followed soon after by the shocking death of my husband, shattered my life, I never imagined that I would ever write about what happened. Those losses left a crater that loomed as large as the Grand Canyon, which I could not enter, and in which I could see hardly anything, like a black hole in space.

Finally, though, I had to look into that darkness, since I could not continue to live fully while refusing to recall what happened, realizing that no one escapes terrible loss. And since everything we experience shapes what we are capable of understanding, I've interwoven this personal story with the work that I love; acknowledging such connections helps us understand the past and illuminate the present.

Many of us, of course, have left religious institutions behind, and prefer to identify as "spiritual, not religious." I've done both—had faith, and lost it; joined groups, and left them. To my own surprise, I then went back, seeking to understand what happened, and to explore how the stories, poetry, music, and art that make up religious traditions have grown out of specific communities and institutions, yet sometimes still resonate.

What matters to me more than whether we participate in institutions or leave them is how we engage the imagination—in dreams, art, poetry, music—since what each of us needs, and what we can engage, obviously differs and changes throughout our lifetime. What fascinates me most are the experiences that shape, shatter, and transform those who initiate or engage them—experiences that precipitate us into new relationships with ourselves and with others. For that, and for you, I offer this writing.

Why Religion?

CHAPTER 1

Why Religion?

William and Louise Hiesey, with Ralph and Elaine, Palo Alto,
California.

On a clear April afternoon when I was fifteen, living at home in Palo Alto, friends from high school invited me to go to San Francisco to hear Billy Graham preach at a giant gathering of his Crusade for Christ. I didn't know what to expect. Why were my friends so eager to see this man? But anything happening in San Francisco promised to be more exciting than a sleepy Sunday among the clipped suburban lawns of Palo Alto. We went early, one of the fathers driving, since we'd heard that huge crowds were streaming to the stadium called the Cow Palace, a basketball arena near Candlestick Park, where I'd seen Willie Mays hit the ball out of the park for a spectacular home run. We were glad to get there three hours early, since now, as then, the bleachers were noisy, densely packed. The *San Francisco Chronicle* reported that eighteen thousand people were jammed inside, while five thousand stood in the parking lot. The roads were blocked with cars for miles in every direction.

When the service finally began, I was amazed to hear Graham's enormous choir singing "washed in the blood of the Lamb," to enthusiastic crowds. Then the moment came, and a handsome, fiery preacher began to speak, quietly at first, warning that what he'd say would sound foolish and irrational to intellectuals and university professors—the authorities in the world I lived in—and it did. He began quoting the prophet Isaiah, "Ah, sinful nation!" Then, increasing his intensity, he scolded America, which some two decades before had dropped atom bombs that killed over a hundred thousand civilians in Hiroshima and Nagasaki, and for driving its most brilliant sons to invent ever-more-horrific nuclear weapons. I was startled, having been taught to admire science as the source of all wisdom, and America as the world's standard of what was right. I'd never heard anyone indict its failings, as he did now. When Graham raised his voice to denounce Christians who used scripture to justify slavery and defend racism while ignoring the poor and our own spiritual poverty, I was riveted. After thundering against America's moral bankruptcy, he paused dramatically and turned, his voice hushed, to speak of our need for God's love, promising everything, including eternal life: all we had to do was go forward and "accept Jesus into your heart."

The preacher's passionate, pleading performance, nearly violent, climaxed in the altar call, as music poured down from hundreds of voices singing praises to God, then the hushed solemnity of the soloist, singing "Just as I am . . ." Billy Graham offered nothing less than a new life. "Born again," I could break out of my family and enter into the family of a heavenly father, who, unlike the earthly one, knew everything about me, even my secret thoughts—yet loved me unconditionally.

This moment, Graham promised, could change everything, could burst the confines of the world in which I'd been living and break through into a new and expansive universe. Having just turned fifteen, I found this invitation irresistible. Moved by his passionate conviction, and overcome with tears, I walked forward toward the speaker with thousands of others to triumphal music, as the choir and the crowd roared approval, praising God for the souls being saved that day. Now all of us who were "born again" shared in a living drama of salvation. That day opened up vast spaces of imagination that I'd previously entered only through the stories and music of others. It changed my life, as the preacher promised it would—although not entirely as he intended, or, at least, not for as long.

My parents were horrified. My father was angry; he hated religion, blaming it for painful conflict in his strict Presbyterian family. When he learned about evolution in college, he'd converted to Darwinism and become a research biologist, certain that the foolish old tales in the Bible appealed only to people who know nothing of science, not to educated people like ourselves. My mother cared little what I thought, but scolded me for upsetting my father. Their reactions scared and secretly pleased me, confirming that I'd struck out to find a different world.

Before then, all I'd known of Christianity was the innocuous brand that infused the white clapboard Methodist church where our mother sometimes took my brother and me for Sunday school. There we would color pictures of Bible stories while I studied the pictures on the walls—Sallman's portrait of Jesus, with fine, feminine hair, blue eyes, harmless and earnest, and another picture of him, his hands clasped on a rock, prayerfully entreating his "father in heaven." We sang of Jesus, who "loves me, this I know," and who "loves the little children of the world; red and yellow, black and white, they are precious in his sight," although those we saw around us in Sunday school were white, except for one Chinese girl.

More fascinating, but strange and frightening, was Saint Aloysius, the nearby Catholic church, where heavy wooden doors swung open into a dark hall that led into a sanctuary lit only with candles flickering before a statue of the Blessed Virgin, her eyes downcast, hands demurely folded. Down the hall, twelve stations of the cross led toward the main altar, gold candlesticks on embroidered white linen, a crucifix suspended overhead, with a wooden body on it, streaked with blood, a crown of thorns pressed into the head of a tortured man who did not look anything like the Methodists' Jesus. I never entered that church alone, but only with my best friend, Jeanne, after we discussed while walking there whatever sins we could think of for her to confess when she disappeared into a black box to whisper to someone hidden behind a screen. I would wait for her to emerge and tell me how many Our Fathers and Hail Marys she would have to say before God would forgive her. I was relieved when we escaped back into the sunlight.

But evangelical Christianity opened up possibilities I hadn't imagined in the life I'd known. A high school friend said that growing up in Palo Alto was like living inside a giant marshmallow, the hard edges—race, poverty, crime—covered with soft, sugary pillows; a place where people go to hide from whatever they want to avoid. I swore a private vow that I'd never again live in one of those comfortable ranch-style houses with concrete sidewalks, in predictable weather—about seventy degrees outside, choice of sun or rain. Where were the ice storms, the snow, the surprises? I would have welcomed even Dr. Seuss's *oobleck*, his fantasy of "something new coming out of the sky." Life in Palo Alto looked pleasant on the surface: "nice" was the operative word—a word I detested.

There *were* hard edges, though, well hidden in our house, with its beige sofa and beige carpets patterned with a rose design. My father was tall and thin, a distinguished scientist, reserved, so soft spoken that you had to lean close to hear what he said, but with bouts of rage that burst out of nowhere, making what I'd heard of land mines underfoot and threats of nuclear war vivid in my dreams. My only defense was silence. Even now, I can hardly speak of those times. During one terrifying explosion, after I had delayed cleaning up after dinner, I thought, "If

I ever go crazy, I would not be screaming. It would be like this—
total shutdown." At other times, his anger was banished underground, but I stepped carefully, aware that it could ignite at any
moment.

I longed to turn to my mother for comfort, but she didn't have
enough for herself, let alone any to share. Fearful and anxious,
she braced herself against the inevitable storm. Physical closeness seemed to embarrass her. My father, also guarded, liked to
tell a story about how he came to know her: in the backseat of her
family's car, while her father was driving on the curving mountain highway toward Santa Cruz. Grandfather drove with abandon, like Toad of Toad Hall, elated and talking enthusiastically,
while thrilling—and terrifying—the rest of us, the car careening
over the highway's center line. On trips like that, they were literally thrown together, stirring embers that flared into desire,
precipitating him into what he'd long resisted: marriage.

Years later I secretly hoarded memories of moments sitting
close to her, when my father was driving, my brother seated next
to him, my mother and me in the backseat; then I could rest my
head on her knees and look out the windows as clouds and tele-
phone poles sped by. At home at night, lying awake in bed, sometimes I could hear her playing Chopin on the piano, the music
embracing me in its harmonies. I collected and hid those moments, having learned early not to confide in her, since looking
to her for understanding invariably put me in the wrong, evoking her blunt stock reply: "You shouldn't feel that way." I was four
when I discovered escalators in a department store, and ran,
shrieking with delight, up and down. This frightened her, and
made her angry; she tried fiercely to stop me. I discovered that
she softened when I was sick, so I often "got sick" on Fridays, so

that I could stay home from school, receive spoonfuls of honey mixed with lemon for a sore throat, look at picture books, and, later, read, basking in her solicitous care.

From her parents, though, my brother and I learned about love. Grandfather was energetic, boisterous, bright, and domineering in the way that came naturally to European men of his generation, but with an exuberant capacity for jokes. I remember him holding me, a small child, tenderly cupping his hands over my feet to keep them warm. A few years later, he showed me how to feed kittens with a doll's baby bottle; and, on my seventh birthday, he and my grandmother thrilled me with a gift of a small dog, which my parents could not refuse. In their summer home near Santa Cruz, Grandfather would make pancakes in the morning, often showing off by flipping them over the rafters, where they sometimes stuck. After that, he played ferocious games of tennis, and challenged us to card games after dinner, laughing when he won—and when he didn't.

He had left his native Holland for America and settled in California, where he found a familiar link to the sea. After working as a carpenter to buy farmland in Saratoga, near Santa Cruz, he built a home, planted orchards of apricots, peaches, apples, and plums, with an abundance of blackberries, strawberries, fresh lettuces, and cucumbers, and invited the young woman he loved to join him there in marriage. Sophie van Druten had been effectively orphaned as a child, after the death of the father she adored, a professor of French at Leiden University. Her mother, addicted after surgery to morphine, then alcohol, was hidden away from her family, the darkest of family secrets. Although I'd assumed that she had died, an uncle told me about the morphine only decades later, suddenly opening a new perspective on what

I'd always taken as my gentle grandmother's naive warnings against drugs and alcohol.

I'd never seen a closer couple. Knowing my grandfather's wild driving in the large green Studebaker he called their "beautiful pea-green boat," I sometimes imagined that if they ever died, they should die together—likely in a car crash. But when she did die, in her late eighties, he was devastated, grieving and raging at the doctors, and we feared he soon would follow. Instead, to our astonishment, he proposed to a close friend of theirs, also widowed after sixty years of marriage, and married her, shocking their other "children," now in their sixties. Knowing how close he and my grandmother had been, I was surprised and moved to see how he, at eighty-seven, could cope with change. Later he told me, "Of course, it's not the same; but still, it's very good."

I never understood how my mother retained her reserve in that family, which seemed to us as welcoming and summery as Grandfather's apricot orchards, so unlike my father's family's deep-shadowed pine forest. Only many decades later, when my mother was in her late eighties, emerging from anesthetic after major surgery and opening her eyes to find me sitting beside her, holding her hand, after flying from New York to be with her, did I see what I'd always longed for: a look of complete love, without a trace of anxiety.

Long before discovering Jesus and Satan, I'd seen *The Wizard of Oz* and read every book about Oz I could find, which plunged me into another world, terrifying and glorious. There, despite my dread of the evil witch, I could roam on my own. To me it all made sense, and helped make sense of the ordinary world: Oz, styling himself "the great and terrible" lord of the land, distant and omnipotent until unmasked, at last, as a "humbug"; the Wicked Witch of the West playing counterpoint with Glenda the Good; the tin man who needs a heart; the scarecrow who wants a brain—and Dorothy, suddenly transported from black-and-white Kansas into a land of color, danger, and excitement, setting forth with only her wits and her dog, Toto. A few years later I discovered another world to explore: Sherwood Forest, where Robin Hood lived as an outlaw with his merry band—Allan-a-Dale, Friar Tuck, and Maid Marian—outwitting the sheriff, dodging and hiding from the evil king's soldiers, while maintaining his loyalty to the absent king who would set everything right, but who came too late.

Stories like those, and poems, music, and dance, evoked what I could imagine only as a spiritual dimension—something not recognized, virtually nonexistent, in the world in which I'd grown up. Stifled in my parents' house, I could breathe more freely when I ran outside to roam with my dog or ride my bicycle to join friends with whom I felt at home. What had started at the evangelical church with "Bible-believing" Christians opened up far more with high school friends who acted at the community theater, where we collected another kind of family—more raucous, playful, and daring. Rehearsing and performing, we imagined ourselves artists, going out for pizza, staying out as late as possible. Often we sang loudly as we drove our friend Richard Stark's car, as he, with his wild, comic flair for conducting and his great bass voice, would lead us in rounds learned in summer camp, popular songs, or Bach choruses like "Jesu, Meine Freude." Sometimes Lowell Clukas, "the poet," would shout, "You've got to hear this," and chant incantations from Dylan Thomas, Baudelaire, or Rilke, or from comic poems made up as we sped along, while Paul Speegle, a painter, gleefully declaimed lines from Nabokov ("Lolita, light of my life, fire of my loins . . .") or from Cyrano de Bergerac ("I love thee beyond life, beyond breath, beyond love's own power of loving!").

Discovering music and poetry with these friends, I also found, through my friend Paul, a world of painting I hadn't known, lit by his spirit and energy. Enjoying his enthusiasm, intensity, and quick intelligence, I responded to his extravagant declarations of love, and his vision of himself as artist, and me as his muse. Paul had quit high school at the age of sixteen, insisting that he hated it, had learned nothing, and wanted only to paint. He collected piles of books on art, especially the Italian painters he loved best: Botticelli, Caravaggio, Piero della Francesca. In the garage at his Atherton home, he stretched canvases, set up easels, tested and mixed paint on wooden palettes, pausing only to read Freud, Dostoevsky, Machiavelli, and anything else he could find. Often he painted furiously until dawn. Paul's father was a well-known drama and music critic for a San Francisco newspaper who took us to the best restaurants in the city, where waiters lavished attention on him, and we could bask, for the moment, in his celebrity. Yet during the times we spent together, Paul often got calls from his younger sister pleading with him to come home right away, telling him that their mother was facedown on the yellow-and-white-tile floor of their elegant home again, dead drunk.

When Paul quit school, his father, frustrated and angry, likely frightened by his son's intransigence, forced him to see psychiatrists, and threatened to commit him to a mental hospital. But the psychiatrists he consulted advised him instead to let his son go on painting, as he did—with stunning talent. That episode shook me: What if his father had succeeded? Were the people whom society called crazy actually misunderstood art- ists, as Paul romantically insisted, or were they "mentally ill," whatever that meant? Troubled by these questions, when I saw that the University of California in Los Angeles was offering a summer college course called "The Sociology of Mental Illness," I applied, hoping to find out.

The next summer, those of us accepted into the seminar lived in dorm rooms at the university. Besides participating in seminar sessions at the university, we took a bus every morning to Camarillo State Mental Hospital, a huge government building built on barren desert land outside Los Angeles where cowboy movies often were shot. Each of us carried keys so that we could sign in on time sheets to any part of the hospital, except violent wards. We also carried pads of lined paper to make notes for af- ternoon meetings, when we'd meet to discuss what we'd seen. The others, except me, were psychology majors, most of them careful to dress in ties or skirts so that no one would mistake them for mental patients. Our teacher, an intense, charismatic Greek sociologist, had challenged us to investigate the effects of hospital procedures on the six thousand patients at Camarillo.

On the first day, after I nervously unlocked the metal door of the ward for "high-functioning" women, I encountered a thin, aggressive young woman who looked me up and down, and asked, "Are you a dyke?" When I said no, she turned abruptly, saying "Damn!" and walked away. I also met Maria, an eighteen- year-old Hispanic girl, nearly my age, with beautiful long, dark curly hair and brown eyes, her arms streaked with razor slash marks, some freshly opened; had the hospital staff not noticed? As we walked back and forth on the concrete floors of the corridors, ignoring the television sets blaring from every corner, she told me how she'd hated the sexual assaults of men in her family and neighborhood; she'd put on a hundred extra pounds to ward them off. Confiding that she was in for repeated suicide attempts, she asked, "Did you ever want to kill yourself?" The question stopped me. After thinking about it, I finally said, "No, but I would if I felt that no one understood me." "That's just how I feel," she said. On a men's ward, one man came up to display a large wound on his arm, which he kept tearing open to show to anyone who would pay attention. I was moved, too, by the young Mormon student, just my age, who spent his days intensely reading a pile of books he'd brought with him, including Darwin's *Origin of Species*, which he'd hidden under a plain brown paper cover. He explained that although he would return to Brigham Young University in the fall, he'd begun to doubt his sanity when he was assailed by "bad thoughts" that impelled him to question his church's teachings.

Later that day, in the admissions office, I joined two other students to observe the procedures. Two hospital workers brought in a man in a straitjacket, unbinding his mouth as he shouted curses at his family members, who followed, ashamed and angry, turning their backs while they signed him in. We were horrified to see the aides forcefully inject him with Thorazine, then wheel him into a treatment room, bind his hands and feet, place him on a table, and administer electric shock that convulsed his body until he went limp. Wasn't this torture?

A few days later, to my surprise, a quiet older woman, gray faced with wispy hair, confessed to me that she periodically signed herself into the hospital for shock treatment—the only way, she said, to ease the horrific anxiety that often confined her to her room. Outside, in the yard, I met a group of men newly released from the army, trading information about various mental hospitals from California to Florida that could guarantee "three squares and a bed" when they chose to migrate during winter. Then I retreated to the ward that housed the children, where a six-year-old girl named Samantha with straight short brown hair, quick and alert as a sparrow, immediately claimed possession of me, demanding to hear stories. After that, I visited her every day to talk and read to her, and she began to learn to read herself. But every day I felt a sinking feeling, realizing that the more she counted on our visits, the harder it would be for her when I left in August, as everyone else had left her, including her mother, who, the aides told me, appeared only rarely, when taking a break from her work as a prostitute.

Our professor explained that he'd intended to become a psychiatrist, but during his residency he'd seen that institutionalizing people, far from helping them, was making them more helpless. He'd designed our course so that we could see this for ourselves. We agreed with much that he said, although the only common denominator I found among the many and various Camarillo residents was that each of them had difficulty living in society. If there were misunderstood artists at Camarillo State Mental Hospital, I didn't meet them; after ten weeks I was relieved to take the bus back to Paul and our circle of friends.

At Kepler's Books in Menlo Park, where we gathered to drink coffee and finger the new books, we met Alan Trist, who'd come from England with his family, and Jerry Garcia, a shaggy-haired musician discharged from the army, who, after riding railroad cars all over the country, was weaving together the disparate strands of American music. Years older than we were, Jerry fascinated us with his daring, and the astonishing range of songs he sang in a gravelly voice, playing lightning-fast changes on his twelve-string guitar, despite having only nine and a half fingers. Now we learned to belt out "Railroad Bill, Railroad Bill / He never worked, and he never will / He just ride, ride, ride"—and heard, for the first time, the music of Appalachia, of Odetta, and Muddy Waters. Years later, Alan startled his parents by becoming the business manager for Jerry's band.

Every Friday I cut classes to spend time with our band of renegades. Four school days a week seemed enough. I was often bored at school, although I enjoyed some classes, and, with a friend, I had started a literary magazine that sold a lot of copies after we recruited several giant football players to hawk it for us. On Fridays, though, my friend Phoebe and I often drove to Los Trancos Woods, for the scent of the grasses, the bay, and the eucalyptus trees, or to the house on Perry Lane, where we found people who looked nothing like the Palo Alto where I'd grown up—more like Robin Hood's band of outlaws.

One day Jerry surprised us, saying that he was getting married—the following Saturday—to someone we'd never seen with him. Arriving at the Unitarian church of Palo Alto, we walked into a church shaped by the late sixties, the traditional cross over the altar replaced by a piece of driftwood. Several rows of Palo Alto high school girls, dressed in pastels, some wearing white gloves, were seated on the left side of the church, the bride's side. On the right, where we sat with the groom's friends, an odd assortment of Jerry's associates gathered in sparse clusters. Jerry shambled in, smiling nervously, his black hair in ringlets around his face as he stared at his feet and glanced quickly at his young and very pregnant bride. The minister concluded the brief service saying, "I now pronounce you man and wife, *as long as this love shall last.*" Hearing these unexpected words, I suppressed a laugh, turning it instead into a sharp intake of breath: How long would *that* be? Afterward, during the reception held at Rickey's Studio Inn on the highway, the waiters refused to serve champagne to the bride, not because she was pregnant—no one thought of that then—but because she was underage.

I still participated every week, sometimes twice a week, in the close-knit group of "Bible-believing Christians" at Peninsula Bible Church on Middlefield Road in Palo Alto, as I had ever since my adolescent passion for evangelical Christianity. As brothers and sisters in Christ, we read the Bible, joined the singing, prayed intensely, and drank grape juice from tiny plastic cups for the "Lord's supper." That passion lasted for more than a year and a half, until the night when Paul, exhilarated while riding as a passenger in a car racing nearly one hundred miles an hour, broke his neck in the crash and died.

When I heard that he'd died, I was speechless, and lingered with our friends as long as possible, afraid to go home. When I did, I was shocked to hear my mother say, "It's for the best; he was no good for you anyway." The emotions roiling around in me suddenly went blind. In an unimaginable universe, I wanted to slug her, punch her face, see her crumple and fall. In the world we inhabited, I stared at her, stunned, then turned and fled to the bathroom, where I vomited until I lay panting on the stone tile. Then I crept quietly to the front door and opened it so that no one would hear, and left. I ran to find a newspaper, fearing it would confirm—as it did—that this thing actually had happened. When I opened the metal box of newspapers and saw the photograph of his face on the front page of every paper, I felt a flash of anger that anyone who casually picked up the paper would see that photo, and so I took them all.

Later, as people gathered at Paul's house, the Episcopal priest came and sat down next to me and quietly asked, "Do you know whether the driver was drinking?" Knowing that he probably was—Lee was a young, angry black army veteran with cancer—I refused to answer. "What difference does that make now?" At the funeral, hearing the priest who stood over Paul's elaborate metal casket call him "a sheep of God's own flock," I flared in defiance: for me he was more the wolf outside than anyone's sheep! By then I'd spent what felt like endless time struggling over whether to walk with the others to look at him for the last time. I was terrified to see his dead face, searing that image into my dreams. For years afterward, I realized the cost of having refused to look into that open coffin; my imagination played havoc with whatever I might have seen, distorted on an internal screen of horrific Halloween nightmares.

My Christian friends, at first sympathetic, immediately asked, "Was he born again?" When I said, "No—he was Jewish!" they said, "Then he's in hell." That made no sense. Wasn't Jesus Jewish? When that didn't seem to matter, I realized that what they said had nothing to do with what had drawn me to that church, and to the faith we'd claimed to share. Instead of drawing people together, as Graham had when he spoke of God's love for everyone, these people were like a club for people spiritually superior to everyone who didn't share their beliefs. Numb, devastated, and alone, I left the church, and never went back.

Starting the day after Paul died, I spent more time with friends who had known him. Richard and I went to the hospital to see Jerry and Alan, who'd survived the crash, as had two others, whom we didn't know. Jerry had shattered the windshield as he was thrown out of the car, which rolled over twice; Alan, also thrown out, had broken his spine. Although by then I was a freshman at Stanford University, I could not concentrate on schoolwork, could barely tolerate what I'd loved: poetry, music, literature. How could these matter now? Instead, I sometimes wandered at night with Richard, Alan, Jerry, and a few others in a straggling group through the fields, talking or silent, then laughing and shouting, watching the night clouds move across the moon. Paul's death had opened up huge questions for all of us—that quick, vivid life suddenly stopped. Where do the dead go? And how to go on living, alert to death's presence, its inevitability?

The following summer, when my high school friend Phoebe and I, as well as Alan and Jerry, moved to San Francisco, what connected us, besides what had happened, was the intense, powerful music we shared, and the apartment that Phoebe and I had rented on Noriega Street, where the others would arrive to sleep on the floor or any available bed after I got up at five A.M. to work in a hospital kitchen, earning money for college next September. When I got home from work around four in the afternoon, they'd be talking. I was startled to hear Jerry saying that now they needed more than music; why not lights and action? I couldn't imagine what he had in mind—surely not opera? And it wasn't; years later, when Jerry's musicians were playing the Fillmore, their performance looked nothing like opera: more like rock dancing in trance. After I left California, when I heard that Jerry Garcia's group of musicians had broken up and that he'd started another band that he called the Grateful Dead, I realized that the name must have resonated from the crash he'd survived five years earlier.

The dark background of those years was formed by violent clashes fought in the streets and played out on television—first civil rights, then the Vietnam War. Those of us who grew up in California's suburban cocoon were shocked to see racial hatred erupt from Arkansas to Berkeley, and to realize that the war was not, as we'd imagined, the patriotic cause publicly preached, but a disastrous blunder, perhaps even a crime. The marine from Camp Lejeune whom I'd occasionally dated in high school, returning to visit California on a short leave, told us how he had gone to 'Nam full of patriotic high feeling, and was horrified when he saw what actually happened there. Like so many others, he never came back, his name later engraved into the stone memorial on the National Mall in Washington, D.C. While Berkeley exploded with political demonstrations, San Francisco burst out in psychedelic fever.

I left Stanford without attending graduation, and, choosing the company of would-be artists, musicians, and poets, set out for New York to take classes at the Martha Graham School on East Sixty-Third Street, intent on devoting myself to dance. I loved the classes that challenged us to turn in spirals, leap, fall, and recover, feeling how Martha Graham's dance evokes myth and ritual. Within a few months, though, I was dismayed, seeing that even the best professional dancers lived almost like nuns, working out like demons, eating nearly nothing, and supporting their uncertain prospects by waiting tables. Had dance been my only passion, I might have done that, but taking classes with members of Graham's company made it clear that I wasn't one of the best, only rather good—and *that* wasn't good enough. What to do next?

To keep options open, I applied to five graduate schools in five different fields. Having loved the work of art historian Meyer Schapiro, I applied to New York University, where he taught; second, I applied to the interdisciplinary program in social thought at the University of Chicago, which sounded fascinating; then to Columbia University's program in English literature, and to Brandeis University, to study with philosopher Herbert Marcuse. What intrigued me most, though, was Harvard's doctoral program in the study of religion, which offered opportunities to study Judaism, Christianity, Buddhism, and Hinduism, so I chose Harvard.

Although I'd left Christianity, questions persisted. Why hadn't religion died out by now—hadn't Nietzsche pronounced God dead a century ago? My father was certain that after people gained a smattering of scientific understanding, they'd shed their Jesus and Moses like shriveled skins. Yet my own experience contradicted that. What made that encounter with evangelical Christianity so powerfully compelling? Was it Christianity, or could any religious tradition evoke such response?

Some things *had* become clear. First, the language spoken in that Crusade for Christ was not spoken in my home—an evocative, emotionally charged language that opened up worlds of possibility, to include legions of angels and archangels, armies of demons, Jesus's bloody sacrifice, a divine someone who heard and understood even the secrets I ferociously protected. After living in a world that felt flat, where emotional intensity was suppressed, in a world devoid of a spiritual dimension, I'd begun to look for a larger life, perhaps on a canvas even bigger than the universe. Although for years I'd loved poetry, from John Donne and Christina Rossetti to Emily Dickinson, Walt Whitman, and C. K. Williams, I began to write poems only after I had entered spaces that those strange, impossible Bible stories opened up, offering paths that led beyond the reach of my family, the beige living room, uncomfortable silences at the dinner table. Among evangelical Christians, I'd begun to find a much larger family, in which people talked freely and passionately, hugged each other, and shouted praises to God because we "loved the Lord."

Now that I'd abandoned that and all other brands of Christianity, I began to wonder how such movements began. Who *was* Jesus? How did the unlikely story of a rural rabbi who preached that the world was coming to an end and God's kingdom was coming, but who himself had come to a cruel and humiliating end, tortured and killed by his enemies, ever become the basis for a worldwide movement still spreading two thousand years later?

How could I find out what really happened, and why it matters? Or *does* it matter? Stanford offered courses from anthropology to zoology, but at the time had no religion department. Instead, the faculty treated religion as a subject unfit for study, except perhaps for Buddhism, which seemed exotic enough not to count as a religion.

Anyone asking questions about Western religion—anyone with a "religious problem"—would be steered toward Stanford's chaplain; but I never went to the office of the Reverend Theodore Good. Religious professionals seemed to be selling different brands of Christianity, nearly all of them insisting that only theirs was right, all others wrong—let alone non-Christians and atheists! For the first time, though, I began to read Greek, and loved the sounds and subtleties of its poetry and drama, which opened a world of gods, goddesses, and monsters that I could never have imagined.

When I visited Stanford, the year after graduating, to talk with my former adviser in Stanford's history department about possible choices, he told me about the Harvard doctoral program in the study of religion, and encouraged me to apply, especially to study with Krister Stendahl, professor of New Testament. I eagerly did so, and, months later, received this response from the professor:

> *Our admissions committee has read your application with interest.*
>
> Ordinarily *we would admit an applicant with your qualifications. However, we are not able to offer a place in our doctoral program to a woman, since we have many qualified applicants, and are able to admit only seven to our doctoral program. In our experience, unfortunately, women students always have quit before completing the degree.*
>
> *However, if you are still serious about pursuing a doctorate next year at this time, we have agreed to offer you admission to our doctoral program for the following year.*

I read that note over and over. *"Still serious?"* They hadn't granted me an interview. Because I'm a woman, did they assume that I'd simply give up? Although deeply upset, I couldn't find another program that looked so promising, and decided to spend another year completing a master's degree in classics at Stanford, continuing to read advanced Greek and Latin, essential for the work I anticipated at Harvard. My father scowled, warning that going to graduate school was a crazy idea for a woman. "If you'd been admitted," he warned, "you'd never get married— you'll turn into one of those lonely women who carry a brief- case and go to the movies alone! No, do something that really makes sense: take typing and become a secretary, or teach in an elementary school." Distressed and discouraged, I stubbornly held to my plan. My grandparents, alarmed at what my parents told them, and knowing nothing of Harvard, much less why any- one would want to study religion, invited me to visit their home among the orchards of Saratoga. They asked many questions, skeptical at first, but listened intently. Finally, my grandfather said, "We don't understand, but you seem to know what you're doing, and you have our blessing." After dinner, when I picked up my plate to take it to the kitchen, I found under it the gift of a hundred-dollar bill.

The following year, I arrived in Cambridge, and made an ap- pointment to meet the formidable Krister Stendahl, a Swedish scholar of fierce intelligence, now to be my first adviser. We met in his office. I was nervous, but also amused that this tall and severe man, wearing a black shirt and clerical collar, looked to me like an Ingmar Bergman version of God. After preliminary formalities, he abruptly swiveled in his chair and turned sternly to ask, "So really, why did you come here?" I stumbled over the question, then mumbled something about wanting to find the es- sence of Christianity. Stendahl stared down at me, silent, then asked, "How do you know it *has* an essence?" In that instant, I thought, *That's exactly why I came here: to be asked a question like that—challenged to rethink everything.*

Now I knew I had come to the right place. I'd chosen Harvard because it was a secular university, where I wouldn't be bombarded with church dogma. Yet I still imagined that if we went back to first-century sources, we might hear what Jesus was saying to his followers when they walked by the Sea of Galilee—we might find the "real Christianity," when the movement was in its golden age. But Harvard quenched these notions; there would be no simple path to what Krister Stendahl ironically called "play Bible land" simply by digging through history. Yet I also saw that this hope of finding "the real Christianity" had driven countless people—including our Harvard professors—to seek its origins. Naive as our questions were, they were driven by a spiritual quest.

We discovered that even the earliest surviving texts had been written decades after Jesus's death, and that none of them are neutral. They reveal explosive controversy between his followers, who loved him, and outsiders like the Roman senator Tacitus and the Roman court historian Suetonius, who likely despised him. Taken together, what the range of sources *does* show, contrary to those who imagine that Jesus didn't exist, is that he did: fictional people don't have real enemies.

What came next was a huge surprise: our professors at Harvard had file cabinets filled with facsimiles of secret gospels I had never heard of—the *Gospel of Thomas*, the *Gospel of Philip*, the *Gospel of Mary Magdalene*, the *Gospel of Truth*—and dozens of other writings, transcribed by hand from the original Greek into Coptic, and mimeographed in blue letters on pages stamped TOP SECRET. Discovered in 1945, these texts only recently had become available to scholars.

This wasn't what I'd expected to find in graduate school, or even what I wanted—at least, not so long as I still hoped to find answers instead of more questions. When I heard of them for the first time, I was tremendously excited, like all of us who were allowed to work on these discoveries, faculty and graduate students alike, in only two universities in the United States: Harvard and Claremont University in California. Historians of Christianity had complained for nearly two thousand years that "heretics," annoying as flies, destructive as killer bees, had plagued the early movement, but nearly everything we knew about them was what their hostile critics wrote. Now, for the first time, the heretics could speak for themselves, and that changed everything.

When I began to read the *Gospel of Thomas*, a list of a hundred and fourteen sayings that claims to reveal "the secret words of the living Jesus," what I found stopped me in my tracks. According to saying 70, Jesus said, *"If you bring forth what is within you, what you bring forth will save you. If you do not bring forth what is within you, what you do not bring forth will destroy you."* Struck by these words, I thought, *We're not asked to believe this; it just happens to be true.* Whether Jesus actually said this, we can't know for sure, but to me that didn't matter. What did matter was the challenge. Before, we had seen only a few fragments of this text, written in Greek; now, for the first time, we could read a complete copy, translated from Greek into Coptic, the language of Egypt nearly two thousand years ago. As I dived into this text, and others, I knew that now I'd have to bring forth—whatever there was to find.

When I first arrived in Cambridge, having arranged a student loan, I'd rented an attic room in an old house on Trowbridge Street near campus, and loved walking through the bizarre jumble of Harvard's architecture. In the seminars, though, I felt somewhat out of place. Nearly every graduate student of religion was male, many of them earnest young ministers, or seeking to be ministers, seriously engaged in academic pursuits. Almost all were safely married—often married young—to women who remained largely invisible, working as secretaries and teachers to support their husbands' graduate school education. The only other woman admitted to our section of the doctoral program, Pheme Perkins, was clearly brilliant. She had previously studied physics, and her no-nonsense exterior suggested that she had rejected traditionally feminine roles to follow her intellectual passion. The ancient university breathed a spirit of having been designed by men and for men, as, of course, it was—not for anomalies like ourselves.

Although feeling lucky to be among the very few women admitted to the doctoral program, I quickly discovered its hazards. Since many of our seminars, even for university students, took place in the Divinity School, where arched ceilings and high windows suggested high-minded and religious thoughts, I often felt like a Dionysian trapped in a church camp. Sometimes, under my breath, I would hum the Rolling Stones' "Sympathy for the Devil"—and also for heretics, since women, too, were cast as outsiders. Then we discovered that several Harvard professors, each of them married, and each with a flock of children, also cast us as sexual targets.

Four weeks after I arrived from California, still awed by Harvard, the short, balding German professor of divinity and reverend minister in the University Lutheran Church, who smoked cigarettes while he taught our introductory class, brusquely informed me that he wanted me to babysit for his four children. Although I had heard that European professors often treat graduate students as unpaid servants, I dared not refuse. That Friday, he picked me up for the thirty-mile drive to the suburb where he lived, then went out with his wife for the evening. When they got back at midnight, he announced that it was too late to drive me back to Cambridge; I'd have to spend the night on a couch in the basement. Cold and unable to sleep, I was startled, two hours later, to hear the door open. The professor crept in toward the couch, groping for my breasts. Suddenly wide awake, I fended him off and ran upstairs to the kitchen—but how to call for help? The only people who could hear me would be his wife and children; calling the police would wake everyone in the house, and he'd simply deny what had happened. There were no cell phones then, and I realized that even if I ran outside at two A.M. into those dark, silent suburban streets, I wouldn't find a taxi or bus, or any way to walk the thirty miles back, even if I'd known which way to go. I stayed awake all night, and in the morning pretended everything was normal. He drove me back without speaking. What shocked me most was to realize how carefully he'd planned his trap. After that, he insisted on being my adviser, and although his predatory attempts continued, I avoided being alone with him.

In the years that followed, this professor became an enthusiastic advocate for admitting women graduate students, on many of whom he honed his new, secret specialty in sexual assault. Decades passed before I dared speak about it. When finally I confided in two women who had been graduate students after me, both, to my surprise, had similar stories about that professor, and another one. After I publicly reported his behavior to a dean in the president's office, I learned that therapists at the Harvard Health Services, themselves bound to confidentiality about what distressed students reported, called him Koester the Molester.

Meanwhile, I struck up a friendship with another oddball—a tall, rakish Texan studying to become an Episcopal priest, who earned money at night and on weekends as a jazz drummer in Boston clubs. His enthusiasm drew me to his church, Boston's Church of the Ascension, an Episcopal church with a dramatic liturgy, framed by the choir singing the ancient anthems of Thomas Tallis and William Byrd, and led by a charismatic priest whose simple, powerful sermons communicated deep engagement with his faith. I approached this kind of worship cautiously, leading at first with the intellect: What *is* this weird ritual cannibalism, eating bread and drinking wine as if they were body and blood? As the strangeness wore off, I was moved to see hundreds of people of every shape, color, size, and disposition, young, old, families, some in Sunday best, others in jeans and sneakers, walk up at the climax of the service to receive a wafer and a sip of diluted wine, until I requested confirmation, and stood up to join them.

Standing in line, I wondered, What kind of hunger drives us to come together, sing, pray, and share a token meal? Are we simply acknowledging a common need? Participating added unspoken depth to what we were learning at the university, from each other and from some of the secret texts we were now reading, written by anonymous Christians who themselves had shared sacred meals thousands of years ago. The anonymous author of the *Gospel of Truth*, another gospel found in the same collection with the *Gospel of Thomas*, says that eating what Jesus offers in that meal—himself—brings joy, as "he discovers them in himself, and they discover him in themselves." Here we found powerfully compelling poetic images of what the *Gospel of Philip* calls "a mystery."

Diving into the secret gospels, though, was exciting: Who wrote them, and what's in them? The discovery of the Dead Sea Scrolls, found two years later, in 1947, already had shaken and radically changed the landscape of the world we hoped to explore. During the first century CE, devout Jews called Essenes (perhaps from the Hebrew term *Hasidim*, or "holy ones"), some of them Jesus's contemporaries, had stored their precious collection of Bible scrolls, prophecies, and sacred texts in caves in Israel, near the Dead Sea. There they'd remained hidden for nearly two thousand years, after Roman soldiers, suspecting the "holy ones" of fighting against Rome, swarmed into their settlement and slaughtered them all. Some of our professors, including Krister Stendahl, along with an international group of scholars, showed how this discovery opens up a much wider, more complex world of radical, devout Jews who, for nearly a hundred years before the first century CE, were predicting the end of time in ways that likely influenced John the Baptist and Jesus.

The nearly simultaneous discovery of the Nag Hammadi library in Egypt came as an even more spectacular surprise. The story we heard told how an Arab farmer named Mohammed Ali, who lived in Nag Hammadi, an Egyptian village about an hour's drive from ancient Thebes (today's Luxor) was digging for fertilizer near a cliff honeycombed with ancient burial caves when he struck something underground and dug up a sealed six-foot jar filled with a stack of ancient books, bound in tooled gazelle leather. Since Mohammed Ali could not read his own language, Arabic, much less the strange script of these books, he took them home and dumped them on the ground near the stove, where his mother later admitted she'd thrown some of the pages into the fire for kindling while she was baking bread. Not long after, while Mohammed Ali and his brothers were in jail, arrested for killing their father's murderer to avenge a blood feud, a local teacher took the texts to Cairo, hoping to sell them on the black market for antiquities. When a dealer there showed the *Gospel of Thomas* to the French scholar Jean Doresse, he began to trace out the first line and was astonished to read, "These are the secret words of the living Jesus, and the twin, Judas Thomas, wrote them down."

Could these be an authentic record of Jesus's sayings? *Did Jesus have a twin brother?* Behind these questions loomed larger ones. We'd heard of secret gospels, but what we knew—or thought we knew—was like what medieval mapmakers imagined beyond familiar continents, where they pictured dragons lurking in uncharted seas. Before this time, none of us had ever seen the *Gospel of Thomas*, except for a few fragments written in Greek, the language of the New Testament. Now, as we investigated these texts for the first time, and struggled to translate them, we graduate students, along with our professors, felt like detectives. I was amazed to find that some of these texts spoke words I'd never heard before yet longed to understand.

Previous generations of historians who'd heard of such secret texts called them "gnostic," since instead of prescribing what to believe, they encourage us to seek *gnosis*. This Greek term, often translated as "knowledge," actually means "insight," or "understanding," since it refers to "knowledge of the heart," which spiritual teachers usually encourage. But as graduate students, we'd already read the writings of Bishop Irenaeus, a Syrian missionary working in rural Gaul (c. 160–180), who warned that Christians offering *"gnosis"* were Satan-inspired heretics. To stanch the flow of their diabolic poison into his congregations, Irenaeus turned *gnosis* into an insult, writing five massive volumes he called *The Destruction and Overthrow of Falsely So-Called Gnosis*, which declared that "the heretics say that they have more gospels than there really are; but really, they have no gospel that is not full of blasphemy."

"So-called gnostics," he charged, lure naive Christians into "unauthorized meetings"—meetings that he, as bishop, hadn't authorized—promising to tell them what Jesus and Paul taught in secret. When the bishop accused these Christians of being "evil interpreters" who simply made up the "secret mysteries" they claimed to offer, they infuriated him, saying that he lacked spiritual insight. Irenaeus retorted that "if someone gives himself up to them like a silly sheep, and follows their practice and their ritual, he gets so puffed up that he walks around strutting, looking superior, with all the pomposity of a cock." They even put forth their own inventions, he says, including "something recently written that they dared call the *Gospel of Truth*, although it's nothing like the New Testament gospels—nothing but an abyss of madness, and blasphemy against Christ!"

When I first read his attack on heretics as a graduate student, knowing Irenaeus's reputation as a respected "father of the church," I assumed that he probably was right. But then I noticed something else: although Irenaeus insists that Jesus and Paul *never* offered secret teachings, the New Testament writings say the opposite. Mark's gospel says that Jesus, like other rabbis of his time, spoke a simple message in public, but explained its meaning only to his closest disciples when he was alone with them, saying, "the secret of the kingdom of God is given to you—

but to those outside, everything is in parables," so that "they may listen, but not understand"—although Mark tells nearly nothing of what he taught in private.

Are the books we're now reading the same ones that Irenaeus denounced? Although we can't know for sure, he *does* mention a *Gospel of Truth*, like the one we now have, which was found at Nag Hammadi in the same collection with the *Gospel of Thomas* and the *Gospel of Philip*. Those who loved and treasured such books, however, didn't think of themselves as "heretics," but as people blessed to have received not only Jesus's public teaching, known to Christians in common, but also his *secret* teaching, which, as we've seen, the *Gospel of Thomas* claims to offer. Many of the texts found with it make similar claims; the *Gospel of Truth*, for example, offers to reveal the secret teaching of the apostle Paul.

Since earlier generations of scholars had no access to what "the heretics" actually wrote, most took Irenaeus at his word and assumed that such teachers were foisting off their own inventions onto naive Christians—"gnostic gospels" that Irenaeus warned them not to read. And while the distinguished group of European scholars who first published the *Gospel of Thomas* didn't find this text as bizarre as they expected, since about half of its sayings also occur in the New Testament Gospels of Matthew and Luke, many assumed that such gospels were opposed to genuine Christian teaching. Even today, you can find dozens of books and articles that treat the *Gospel of Thomas* as an alien text, and interpret it as "gnostic" heresy.

The more we looked in these secret texts for answers, the more questions opened up. Even a first dive into them showed that what we call "Christianity" is a huge, messy heap of traditions, stories, images, and practices, collected by people all over the world—much that may be of value, and much that may not. When I began to sort these out, a "Bible-believing" Christian warned me that: "Picking and choosing is self-indulgent. We call it cafeteria Christianity," he said, "since people who do that simply refuse to accept the whole tradition as it stands." In a sense, of course, he's right. Ever since the second century, Christian leaders calling themselves orthodox ("straight thinking") have defined choice as *heresy*. The Greek term translated as "heresy" (*hairesis*) means exactly that: "choice"!

So we're still asking, "How did these texts end up buried, unknown for nearly two thousand years?" Now we're beginning to see some pieces of the puzzle come together. Nearly two hundred years after Irenaeus waged war on "heretics" and their gospels, another powerful bishop named Athanasius, bishop of the Egyptian city of Alexandria, ordered Christians all over Egypt to reject what he called "illegitimate, secret books." But although monks in the central monastery copied out Athanasius's order in large letters on a wall where everyone could see it, some monks apparently defied the bishop's orders, and removed over fifty texts from the library that held their sacred books, sealing them into a heavy jar, and hiding them under the cliff near Nag Hammadi, where Mohammed Ali said he found them sixteen hundred years later.

That's lucky, since some of us need heresy—*choice*, that is. The collection of traditions that includes everything from the stark and simple *Gospel of Mark* to the prayers and hymns of Saint Francis, Saint Bernard, and Hildegard, along with stories of martyrs and wild-eyed saints, all kinds of music, dozens of "rules" for various Christian communities, poems of John of the Cross, George Herbert, John Donne, Gerard Manley Hopkins, Emily Dickinson, and Dylan Thomas, as well as decrees that countless church councils forged centuries ago, diatribes, polemics, heavy volumes weighed down with centuries of theological debate—and now a whole library of censored "heretical" writings—is overwhelming. No one can swallow it all; it's indigestible.

Instead, in each generation, leaders, from the apostle Paul to Martin Luther King Jr. and Saint Mary of Paris, have selected elements from that vast collection, discarding some and reinterpreting others, focusing on those that deal with the specific challenges each one faces. Far from destroying Christian traditions, this selection process enables them to survive, adapt, and spread, even today, in radically different cultures as new situations unimaginable in previous generations arise. Yet nearly every group, from Roman Catholic, Baptist, Pentecostal, Mormon, Methodist, Christian Scientist, Quaker to Ethiopian Orthodox, tends to claim that its version of Christianity is the only right one, the only one that goes back to Jesus himself.

"Am I religious?" Yes, incorrigibly, by temperament, if you mean susceptible to the music, the rituals, the daring leaps of imagination and metaphor so often found in music, poems, liturgies, rituals, and stories—not only those that are Christian, but also to the cantor's singing at a bar mitzvah, to Hopi and Zuni dances on the mesas of the American Southwest, to the call to prayer in Indonesia. But when we say "religion," what are we talking about?

Like most people, I used to think that religion was primarily a matter of "what you believe." But I've had to abandon that assumption, since seeing how the particular circumstances of

Christianity's origin led certain leaders to equate "true religion" with a set of beliefs, especially since the fourth century, when certain bishops hammered out the list of doctrines called the Nicene Creed, and Emperor Constantine and his successors decided to use it as a test of who is—or isn't—legitimately religious. Even today, many Christians insist on a single set of beliefs— whichever one their denomination endorses.

What I love about sources like the *Gospel of Thomas* is that they open up far more than a single path. Instead of telling us what to believe, they engage both head and heart, challenging us to "love your brother as your own life," while deepening spiritual practice by discovering our own inner resources: "Knock upon yourself as on a door, and walk upon yourself as on a straight road. For if you walk on that road, you cannot get lost; and what you open for yourself will open."

While urging us to seek a deep connection with reality, they encourage us to walk without a map, expecting turbulence and surprise: "Let the one who seeks not stop seeking until he finds; and when he finds, he will be troubled; when he is troubled, he shall be astonished." And when asking where to start, we find another saying from the *Gospel of Thomas*: "Recognize what is before your eyes, and the mysteries will be revealed to you."

CHAPTER 2

Love and Work

Heinz and Elaine Pagels, on their wedding day, New York City.

Gray skies and damp wind, early spring in Cambridge, on the day I flew back to California, grateful to walk off the plane and see blue skies, feel light breeze, smell the eucalyptus. I'd come to see my grandfather, now ill, who would linger only a few more weeks. I drove straight to the hospital and found his room. He clasped my hands to his chest and held them, his voice rasping in his dry throat, and said, "Where's your husband?" Startled, I wondered, Now that I'm twenty-three and not married, is he saying that my eccentric choices are taking me away from what means everything to him? What I could not have imagined is that this trip would answer his question.

Several days later, driving up to Los Altos Hills to see Mike Schick, a tall, good-humored, red-bearded physicist, and Pamela, his wife, a dancer, I was surprised to see another physicist, whom I'd met at Stanford, now visiting from New York. I'd first seen him when I was seventeen, when he walked into the coffee shop in Palo Alto called Saint Michael's Alley, a tall young man with a radiant smile. Stunned, I turned to my high school friend and whispered, "Do you see that beautiful young boy?" A year later, when I was a freshman at Stanford, we met. His name was Heinz Pagels, and he told me that on the day I'd first seen him he'd just driven from Pennsylvania through the Sierra Nevada mountains to the sea, to begin graduate study in physics at Stanford. When we did meet, I didn't tell him how I felt, of course, since I was going out with someone else, and I already knew two of his former girlfriends. At the time, he liked to say that he was a serial monogamist—and I felt far too susceptible to become another episode!

During our years at Stanford, we'd seen each other only in

passing, most recently before I left California for Harvard. He
and his roommates were giving one of their Saturday-night parties, when they would drive to the coast to get abalone, then
cook spaghetti and spread a red-checkered tablecloth on the
floor to serve dinner, before clearing everything away to dance.
Heinz and I flirted often, and loved to dance—he was tall and
agile, a marvelous dancer. That evening, as we were dancing,
he teased me, saying, "Why are you going to Harvard? You're
going to price yourself right out of the market!" While dancing,
amused and annoyed, I replied, "I'm not in any market, thank
you very much," thinking, *If a man this attractive and intelligent
says something* this *stupid, what hope is there for the rest of the
male species?* But then, with his most charming smile, he said,
"I'll make a deal with you: I won't get married for five years, if
you don't," and I laughed, finding him irresistible as ever. When
I left for Cambridge, he went on a trip around the world with his
current girlfriend, giving physics talks from Japan and China to
Cambodia and the Himalayas in India, before returning to join
the faculty at New York's Rockefeller University.

Now, on this spring evening in California, five years later, we
were meeting again. We sat close together and talked for hours.
As I was leaving, he invited me to New York; I invited him instead to the Princeton–Harvard football game in Cambridge
in the fall. That October, I was excited that he came, and we
enjoyed the day, absorbed far more in each other than in football. At dinner, he challenged me: "Why *religion*, of all things?
Why not something that has an impact in the real world?" Good
question—one I'd been asking myself—but why did he love the
physics of virtually invisible elementary particles: hadrons, bo-
sons, and quarks? After an intense discussion, contentious and

hilarious, we came to see that each of us was hoping to understand something fundamental. I began to see what fascinated him about investigating the natural world, from the "big bang," to elementary particles and galaxies; and he became intrigued with the secret gospels. That evening, as he kissed me goodnight, I impulsively said, "Don't go"—and he immediately agreed, sat down and took off his shoes. Years later, when we traveled to Egypt, Israel, and Sudan, we both began to see how ancient traditions as familiar—or strange—as those biblical stories *do* have impact, even now, in our world.

During those first few days we discovered that we could not be apart, and began traveling every weekend between New York and Cambridge; he'd carry a small suitcase packed with books to read on the way. I'd never felt so close to anyone, loving his open, enthusiastic embrace of new experiences, his instinctive generosity, his quick insight and wit, and the warmth of his arms around me. The following spring, when Harvard offered me a year's fellowship to study at Oxford, I secretly hoped he'd say "Don't go; stay here with me." Instead, to my disappointment, he said, "I don't know much about love, but I know it doesn't tie people down," so I went. Since we'd hardly dared speak of love, let alone of a future together, I resolved to forget him, or try to. But when I arrived in England, the moment I stepped out of the train at the Oxford station and saw a billboard advertising canned soup that read "Heinz Souperman," I laughed and nearly cried; already I'd failed to forget him! A few weeks later, having agreed to go out with an intriguing American student who wore a black leather jacket and offered me a ride on his motorcycle, I burst into tears because he wasn't Heinz.

During Christmas break, Heinz invited me to New York,

taking me to his family home in Pennsylvania to celebrate Christmas and to meet his widowed mother. Clearly, this was a test. I was nervous. I was relieved to meet a beautiful, stately, and reserved woman, who firmly placed us in separate rooms; we all pretended that this was normal. After we returned to his New York apartment on Friday, the week after New Year's Day, he was unusually quiet. Then he put his arms around me, and asked me to marry him. At first I didn't reply, since we'd never talked about marriage. After a few moments, nervously, he said, "You may need time to think about it." Finally I found my voice, and said, "There's nothing to think about; I'm just surprised you asked!" That afternoon we walked in the snow that had been falling steadily all day, transforming Central Park into a brilliant, unfamiliar wilderness. When we reached the Museum of Natural History and walked through the halls of dioramas, each showing pairs of male and female antelope, kudu, and herons, I felt complete, like an animal who'd found her mate.

When I told my adviser—the one who'd repeatedly tried to seduce me—that we were going to marry in June, he exploded. "You *what*? You're one of our best students; *we've wasted four years on your education, and you're getting married?*" Astounded that he took this to mean that I was quitting graduate school, I stopped myself from saying, *You've wasted what?* And said only, "Whenever one of the *men* says that he's getting married, you say, 'Good—now you'll settle down.'" He was so adamant—both of us aware of his previous advances—that he tried to cut off the Harvard scholarship that supported me; but this time Krister Stendahl, now the dean, stopped him.

What kind of wedding? At the time, many people we knew were reinventing rituals, choosing to marry in exotic places, in hot-air balloons, on mountaintops, sometimes on psychedelics, writing their own vows. Although Heinz had no liking for churches, he said, "People who write their own vows are trying to control what's happening to them; but getting married takes us beyond anything we can control." I suggested the archaic vows of the Episcopal prayer book service ("With this ring I thee wed; with my body I thee worship."), a service that reminded me of the stone doorways at Oxford, worn down by people who'd entered them for hundreds of years. He agreed, since it would be short, just ten or fifteen minutes. But how could we invite our friends, since most of them had nothing to do with religious services? We asked the organist to play Bach quietly, at first, as people were entering the small Church of the Resurrection on Seventy-Fourth Street in New York, creating a spacious harmony, then gradually building to glorious chords that led into the short, simple ceremony. After that, we all went to Rockefeller University on the East River, where a rock band was warming up to play, for a joyful evening with close friends and family, hugging, laughing, and dancing.

After a welcome weekend by the sea in Providence, we flew to California, where physicists had invited Heinz to engage in research with them for the summer, while I would continue writing my dissertation. As we drove up to the apartment that the Stanford Linear Accelerator staff assigned to us for summer housing, I was shocked into silence. In a city of over sixty thousand people, they'd rented for us the same apartment where I'd so often been with my friend Paul, the apartment where his grandmother had lived. As we walked up the stairs into the familiar living room, I suddenly felt that Paul was present, invisible, standing near the window that overlooked the garden.

Astonished, I resisted an impulse to turn and run, wondering, *Is he actually here?*—or, as seemed more likely, in my imagination? In a flash I realized that I could not tell—and that it didn't matter. What *did* matter was how to respond. Instinctively I spoke to him internally, saying, "You are welcome here." At that moment I felt the presence depart. Too startled to tell Heinz about it then, I told him much later.

Heinz, too, was fascinated by qualities of consciousness, often wondering, as he put it, "When we do physics, are we actually discovering elementary particles, or just creating mathematical constructs?" Hearing him talk, I began to appreciate how physicists invent images of particle interaction—glue, string, n-dimensional space—and how physicists interweave imagination with close analysis of data. He also liked to have lunch at the Stanford Research Institute to talk with scientists there about their experiments testing mental telepathy, distance vision, and extrasensory perception. Years before, as a graduate student, having heard that scientists at Palo Alto Veteran's Hospital were offering volunteers seventy-five dollars to participate in a double-blind experiment in which each participant would receive either a placebo or LSD, he'd promptly volunteered. What he took "wasn't a placebo," he told me later, saying how astonished he was to see stars and galaxies being born and dying, while others emerged, through what felt like innumerable ages. Although he didn't take LSD again, the summer after we married he encouraged me to try it, promising to cope with any difficulty that might arise.

When I did, we anticipated that what would happen might involve what I was writing about, some kind of Christian vision. Instead, as I sat in the apartment, looking out at the sky, the trees in light wind, and the garden, I saw everything alive as fire, gloriously intertwined. Watching, ecstatic and speechless, for about five hours, I finally managed to say, "I guess that solves the dying problem," and he laughed. What had horrified me before, when Paul died—that a beloved person could simply disappear, and disintegrate—now seemed to resolve into a deeper unity of the whole.

That fall, returning to Cambridge, I worked hard to complete doctoral exams and finish the dissertation, and was relieved and happy to graduate with distinction. Our closeness felt like a refuge, a source of joy, encouraging each of us to try new things. We found a small rent-controlled apartment, the top floor of a brownstone near Central Park West, and I was excited to begin teaching in September. While beginning to teach, I wrote two scholarly books and several articles, and continued doing what I loved best, working with a group of nearly thirty scholars to translate, edit, and publish more than fifty texts from Nag Hammadi: a quickly done English translation first, and then a scholarly edition in five volumes, which would take decades to complete. But as we struggled to translate from Coptic and write detailed notes on every line, sometimes every word, I kept thinking, "Just publishing these isn't enough. Like the Bible, these ancient texts are hard for people to pick up and read. How can we show what a difference these texts make—how they change our perspective on *everything*?" That question wouldn't go away, and eventually it impelled me to write a book I called *The Gnostic Gospels*.

As we plunged into a new life in New York, I began to teach at Barnard College, a school for women built in 1889, when women were excluded from Columbia University, which its founders built in 1754 to educate men. As I arrived in 1970, women were starting to challenge traditional gender roles, energized by the civil rights movement, which had demanded the equality America claimed to offer, but didn't. Colleagues at Barnard who initiated our first conference on women asked me to participate, saying, "Just talk about women in the early Christian movement." At first I said no, repeating what I'd learned about women at Harvard—*nothing*! "We don't have enough information." After all, hadn't men written almost everything we'd read? Of course, we couldn't know; but what we knew of ancient education made that seem likely. When I asked a favorite professor, George MacRae, who'd written an article on the story of Eve, he said with surprise, "Why ask me? How should I know?" He was right: Why ask MacRae, a Jesuit priest?

While thinking about the conference, I suddenly realized that although the sources in the New Testament often marginalize women and minimize their roles, the secret gospels and other texts found in Egypt—some, especially—abound in feminine images, even for God. None of my male colleagues had noticed this, and I hadn't either, until I had been asked to confront the question. The *Secret Revelation of John*, for example, opens as the disciple John, devastated by Jesus's death, goes out into the desert alone to grieve, when suddenly "the whole creation shone with light, and the world was shaken." Terrified, John says he heard Jesus's voice speaking from that light, saying, "John, John, why do you weep? Don't you know that *I am with you always? I am the Father; I am the Mother, and I am the Son!*" Suddenly, I thought, "Of course—who *else* would you expect to find with the *father* and *son* but the *mother*?" Anyone reading the Bible in Hebrew would see that the words "spirit" (*Ruah*) and "wisdom" (*Hokmah*) are feminine, and might easily envision the spirit, or wisdom, as feminine aspects of God—divine mother. Furthermore, nearly two thousand years ago, Bishop Irenaeus denounced "heretics" who, he complained, were teaching people in his congregation to pray "in the name of the unknown Father, and in the name of Truth, the Mother of all being." As I began to piece together the evidence, the hidden contours of censored forms of Christianity were taking shape.

So when asking, "What difference does it make how we imagine God?" I realized that Israel's god was an anomaly—a single male god, who, unlike other male gods among his contemporaries, had no feminine partner, as in Egypt, where Isis and Hathor were worshipped along with Ra and Horus, or in Greece or Rome, where Zeus and Jupiter were paired with divine wives, sisters, and lovers, like Hera and Juno. And while many Jewish, Christian, and Islamic theologians say they don't think of God in sexual terms at all, the language in which they pray and worship every day sends the opposite message. Who, raised as a Jew, Christian, or Muslim, escapes the impression that God is *masculine*? Even when Jesus's followers broke with Jewish tradition to speak of one God in "three persons," they pictured two of those divine "persons"—Father and Son—as masculine, and the third, the Spirit, as sexless, since in their language, Greek, the word "spirit," feminine in Hebrew, is gendered neuter (*pneuma*), and later was translated into Latin as the masculine word *spiritus*.

Fascinated with what now was becoming obvious, I agreed to speak at the Women's Conference at Barnard. To my delight, on the day it began, Heinz showed up, one of a handful of men amid thousands of women, wearing a huge WONDER WOMAN button that someone at the meeting had given him. I told stories from the secret texts—for example, telling how startled God was when his mother, the Spirit, divine Wisdom, scolded him for showing off:

> Becoming arrogant in spirit, [he] boasted over everything below him, saying, "I am father, and God, and there is no one above me!" But when he said this, he sinned against the whole of being. And a voice came forth from above— *the voice of his mother, divine Wisdom!*—saying, "You are mistaken, Samael," [that is, "blind god"]. "Do not tell lies!"

Two thousand women roared with laughter, then listened intently as the *Secret Book of John* went on to tell how "the Blessed One, the Mother-Father, the blessed and merciful one ... sent ... a helper to Adam, the luminous *Epinoia* ['creative intelligence'] who comes forth from him, who is called Life [*Eve*]—the one who is to awaken his thinking."

Texts like the *Secret Book* sometimes turn traditional readings of the biblical story upside down. Certain rabbis, playing on a pun in Hebrew between "Eve" and the word "teacher," blamed Eve for teaching Adam to sin, and pictured the Lord scolding her, saying, "The serpent was your serpent, and you were Adam's serpent"; but some of the Nag Hammadi texts see her instead as Adam's *spiritual* teacher. The *Testimony of Truth* tells how "divine intelligence" first spoke to Adam through Eve, and then through the serpent, encouraging the first man and woman to eat from the tree of knowledge, so that they could break free from the tyranny of the Lord, the garden's master, who'd threatened them with death, and threw them out of Eden. So, this author concludes, "What kind of God is this? Surely he has shown himself to be a malicious envier!" Some versions of this story insist that it was not the Lord God, as the *Genesis* story suggests, but his evil underlings who punished Eve by establishing male domination, telling her that "your desire shall be for your husband, and he shall rule over you."

Conference participants clapped and shouted, all of us surprised that the anonymous authors of these previously unknown texts had challenged traditional gender roles thousands of years before we'd begun to do so ourselves. Yet even then, some "orthodox" Christians pushed back hard. The second-century African convert Tertullian, echoing Bishop Irenaeus, warned that women are especially attracted to heresy—dangerously so, he said, because it encourages them to defy male authority. In his *Prescription Against Heretics*, he writes:

> These heretical women—how audacious they are! They
> have no modesty; they are bold enough to teach, to engage
> in argument, to practice exorcism, to enact healing, and,
> it may be, even to baptize!

Enthusiasm and laughter showed that we'd hit a raw nerve. Probably every woman participating had experienced men's efforts to suppress her and impose the male domination that biblical stories often endorse. Unexpectedly, then, this dive into the sources had plunged us into social history, showing that precisely because the creation stories *are* old folktales, they effectively communicate cultural values that taught us to "act like women." Besides revealing how such traditions pressure us to act, these stories also taught us to accept the role of women as "the second sex," a phrase that Tertullian coined in the second century. The same Christian leaders whose scriptures censor feminine images of God campaigned to exclude women from positions of leadership, often hammering on the Bible's divine sanction of men's right to rule—views that most Christians have endorsed for thousands of years, and many still do.

My experience at the conference changed my perspective. At Harvard, we'd been told that controversies over heresy were arguments over conflicting *ideas*. But now that I'd seen how issues of sexuality and gender—or of any ideas that matter—are inextricably interwoven with how we live, what we choose, and how we set up a society, the history of ideas opened up, so to speak, into three dimensions. Those who struggled to shape the early Christian movement were contending with urgent and practical questions: Who's in charge? Whose authority do we accept? Can women lead, or only men? If arrested for being a Christian, should you admit it and accept a sentence of death, or dodge the question and survive? To what group, if any, do you belong? With which group do you identify? Who chose the gospels now included in the New Testament, and why? Who's in, who's out—and who has the right to say?

Now that the people whom traditionally minded scholars dismissed as "the crazies" could speak for themselves, we could include their voices in the conversation. From now on, instead of writing primarily about *ideas*, I'd have to show how ideas are inseparably woven into actual social codes, and so into behavior. Although no one, so far as I knew, had ever read these sources that way, now I had to, and so began the research that eventually would lead to the book I wanted to write.

To my delight, Heinz shared my enthusiasm. While writing his own book, *The Cosmic Code: Quantum Physics as the Language of Nature*, he joked that we should write a book together, scrambling our titles—either "The Cosmic Gospels" or "The Gnostic Code." I realized then, even more now, how much I owe to this loving, openhearted man. I started by doing what I learned in graduate school: writing a set of scholarly articles for academic journals. But because our friends would never read those, Heinz encouraged me to do more. Why not rewrite those scholarly articles—*translate* them, so to speak—into accessible language, so that people who aren't scholars could see how these secret gospels are changing everything we used to think or thought we knew?

When I did, I was amazed that Jason Epstein, a brilliant editor but no fan of religion, found the story intriguing and decided to take a chance on it. He arranged to publish it at Random House, after excerpts first appeared in *The New York Review of Books*. Having already published two scholarly books in the formal academic style I'd learned at Harvard, I now began to consider the questions raised at the Barnard conference and say what I actually thought in the book that became *The Gnostic Gospels*.

Excited and nervous, I knew that the book would be controversial—and it was. Immediately a review appeared on the front page of the Sunday *New York Times Book Review*, written by Raymond Brown, a renowned senior colleague and biblical scholar. After opening with cautious praise for my reputation, since he knew me as a colleague and had invited me to participate in writing a book with him and others, he attacked the secret gospels, declaring that since they were only rubbish in the first century, and were still rubbish, what I'd written could only deceive the public! Next, my mentor at Oxford, Henry Chadwick, a prominent Anglican professor and clergyman, wrote a strongly worded attack in the *London Review of Books*, repeating what the church fathers had said thousands of years ago, that Gnostics were essentially not Christian at all. He finished with scolding words the Bible attributes to the apostle Paul—that women, weaker than men and less rational, are easily seduced by heresy. A third colleague, Joseph Fitzmyer, published "The Gospel According to Pagels" in the Jesuit journal *America*—an attack so mocking and vituperative that other colleagues urged me to sue him for libel.

After those first attacks and several enthusiastic positive reviews, buckets of mail arrived, packed with letters of intense appreciation, and others seething with hate, threatening hell and damnation. I stuffed them together into a large cardboard box, which I later misplaced and never found. To my surprise, the sensation that the book caused helped release me from worrying about what others would say, since neither the praise nor blame mattered as much as I had imagined they would—and mattered far less than finding my own voice.

During the Barnard conference, Sharon Olds, a close friend from Stanford, introduced me to Elizabeth Diggs, a playwright then completing her doctoral dissertation in Columbia's English Department. Since we all loved to dance, the three of us met every week, first with a dance teacher, then by ourselves at Lizzie's downtown studio, to explore improvisational dance, an ongoing, intricate conversation in movement. As our friendship grew, I became aware that I felt erotically attracted to Lizzie, who spoke openly about relationships with both men and women. Married and divorced twice in her twenties, she now declared herself bisexual, and was living with a woman she loved. While this attraction held no threat either to my marriage or to our friendship, even acknowledging it made me uncomfortable. Yet I knew—hadn't we all read Freud?—that such feelings were virtually universal. Why had I, or any of us, unthinkingly accepted what didn't make sense, and contradicted our own experience? How, I wondered, had sexual attitudes about marriage, divorce, homosexuality, and abortion that we'd grown up with—all of them now rapidly changing—been made to feel as natural as if they'd been built into the structure of the universe? How had we not been aware of how culturally conditioned those attitudes are? What happened at the Women's Conference offered some clues; travel in Africa would soon suggest more.

Shortly after *The Gnostic Gospels* was published, those of us working on the secret gospels eagerly accepted an invitation to participate in the first international conference on Coptic studies in Cairo. Despite the sagging metal mattress frames and the rats scampering through our rooms on cement floors at night at the Garden City House hotel, we got up early to go to the Coptic Museum. There, for the first time, we were excited to see what we'd known only from photos: the actual texts, startlingly beautiful, written in black ink on papyrus, golden brown as tobacco leaves, so fragile that they'd been pressed between sheets of plastic to keep them from shattering. The next day we drove to the village in Upper Egypt where a team of archaeologists, working with men from the village, were excavating a large monastic compound—the site of one of the earliest monasteries built in Egypt, around 315 CE. Monks from that monastery may have been the ones who hid the "secret books" denounced by the bishop, taking them out of their sacred library, carefully sealing them into a six-foot jar, and hiding the jar where Mohammed Ali, the villager who claimed to have discovered it, said he found it, buried under a nearby mountain honeycombed with caves. For millennia, Egyptians had buried the dead in those caves, where, centuries later, monks would retreat to pray and meditate. Even now, nearly two thousand years later, when entering a large cave, I could read the first line of a psalm ("I will lift up my eyes unto the hills, whence comes my help"), which someone, likely a monk, had written on the wall in large Coptic letters, to prompt those who retreated there to pray and recite the psalm they would have known by heart.

When Arab workmen took time off from the dig to celebrate the holy days of Ramadan, we took a taxi down to the Valley of the Kings, descending from blazing sunlight into the cool of the tombs, marveling at a painting of the divine Isis spreading her protective wings across the ceiling, and another of the goddess Nut, her dark body spangled with stars, bending over the night sky. Toward evening, on the way back to the sugar factory where we were staying, military police blocked the road and ordered us to stop. That afternoon, a decades-long blood feud between families on opposite sides of the road had erupted into machine-gun firefights, which had already damaged several cars. We returned to Luxor, where our director negotiated with the police, offering several cartons of Marlboros and a bottle of Johnnie Walker, then contraband in Egypt. A few hours later, the mayor of Luxor provided us with a military escort, machine guns at the ready, pointing out the taxi windows. As we got closer to the crowds by the roadside, terrified by the shouting and gunshots, I dived to the floor of the car, greatly amusing my male colleagues, who insisted that they loved the adventure, and have joked about it ever since.

As the conference concluded with a lavish dinner given by

members of the Coptic community, and hosted by the stately, black-bearded Coptic pope, Shenouda III, Heinz arrived, and we flew together to Israel. In Jerusalem, after attending meetings of the Einstein Centennial in the Old City, and seeing colleagues at the Hebrew University, we drove to the Weitzmann Institute to drive with Heinz's physicist friends into the Sinai desert. Traveling in army jeeps by day, and camping at night under brilliant stars, we reached Mount Sinai, where biblical legend says Moses saw the burning bush and received the Torah from the Lord himself. Near camps where Bedouins were cooking lentils and roasting lamb, monks from the ancient monastery of Saint Catherine still preside over what they say is the oldest Greek monastery in the world, built among the red rocks below the mountain.

Since we were on our way to Africa, friends in Jerusalem asked us to bring gifts to children of a friend of theirs, a Sudanese woman whose husband had died in a car accident in Cambridge while she was completing her law degree. Now a distinguished professor of law at the University of Khartoum, she invited us to lunch at the faculty club, while her uncle and brother sat silently at our table. We were startled to hear her explain that although she was not a strict Muslim, Sharia law would not allow her to host a male visitor, even accompanied by his wife, without male relatives present. There, too, we met with Francis Deng, a tall, elegant man, then minister of state for foreign affairs of Sudan, who showed us a book he'd written as a student at King's College London, a collection of stories traditional among his people, the Dinka. What impressed me most about Dinka creation stories was how *practical* they are: they show people how to live, what matters, what to do, and what to avoid.

Weeks later, emerging from many days of camping near the

Uganda border, dreaming of hot showers, we enjoyed the luxury of a night's stay at the Khartoum Hilton, where, in the lobby, I found a worn copy of *Time* magazine, and read it from cover to cover. What fascinated me most were letters to the editor protesting a previous lead story on bisexuality in America. To my surprise, four out of six of those letters invoked the *Genesis* creation story to prove that only heterosexuality is "natural" and "right." Reading them right after the Dinka stories, I began to see that what my father had dismissed as foolish old folktales are not, as he assumed, simply "science for dummies"—stories that "primitives" tell to explain the creation of the natural world. Instead, creation stories help create the *cultural* world, by transmitting traditional values. And although I hadn't been brought up to take the *Genesis* stories literally, the discomfort I'd felt acknowledging any attraction for a woman showed me that I'd absorbed, quite unconsciously, the cultural messages the Adam and Eve stories have conveyed for thousands of years. On the flight back to New York, I kept wondering, *Why do people continue to tell such stories to this day? What do these stories mean to them?*

After we arrived back in New York, as our taxi passed activists picketing Saint Patrick's Cathedral to protest Catholic opposition to homosexuality, the driver turned to us and said, "You know, as I see it, God made Adam and Eve, not Adam and Steve!" Yes, we *did* know. Amazing, I thought—a bad joke, but one that shows how this story still works as a cultural Rorschach test, to which countless people, religious or not, reflexively turn when they encounter something that makes them uncomfortable. For creation stories claim to tell how the world was *meant* to be, or how it *should* be—how it was in the beginning. Now I was eager to explore how, for thousands of years, various people have read this story that explains so little and suggests so much: the Lord plants a special garden, where he places a naked man and woman, newly made; luscious fruit that can make you wise or kill you; then the garden's master threatens them with death if they touch it, while a talking snake urges them on.

When I first studied Hebrew, starting with *Genesis*, I was surprised to learn that the Bible includes not one, but *two* creation stories—not only the folktale of Adam and Eve, but *another* creation story, placed right before it, which begins "in the beginning," and tells how God created the world in seven days. Like so many others, my father had mistaken this story for primitive science, having heard it from people who took it literally. Back in New York, I began to reflect on why people tell such stories. Reading the biblical creation story this time, I could see that it is not so much about how God created nature, but how such stories created a *culture*: how, for example, this story speaks of the world as originally "good," intelligently planned by a beneficent creator, thus teaching its readers to celebrate the world's beauty, and worship its creator. And by telling how God worked for six days, then rested, the story teaches its hearers that they, too, should work for six days and rest on the seventh, the holy day of Sabbath—a ritual that marks them as God's people, set apart from "the nations."

I was excited to see that our creation stories are as practical as those of the Dinka. Whether we believe them or not, they are transmitted in our cultural DNA, powerfully shaping our attitudes toward work, gender, sexuality, and death. The first story, for example, tells how God first commands the original human couple to use their sexual energy: "Be fruitful, and multiply, and fill the earth!" Reading this now, we can see that much in the Bible that sounds strange, or at least alien to contemporary values, makes much more sense when we understand the situation of the people who first told these stories. This first creation account, likely told and retold long before it was written down some three thousand years ago, transmits the cultural code of nomadic people, whose survival and well being depended on fertility, too precious a resource to waste—not only the fertility of their herds of goats and sheep, but also of themselves. The legal codes now bound with *Genesis* into the Hebrew Bible reinforce that primary command, treating any *nonprocreative* use of sexual energy—for example, sexual relations with someone of the same gender or with a prostitute, or spilling semen on the ground—as "abominations to the Lord," some of which could get you killed.

So while nothing feels more personal and private than our sexual responses, how we experience them may have a lot to do with what we inherited from ancient Israel. Even the laws that criminalize sexual activity between men name it "sodomy" from a story in *Genesis* 19, which says that God sent the volcanic eruption that destroyed the ancient city of Sodom to punish and kill every man in that city, "down to the last man," for having sex with other men. This story pictures Lot pleading in vain with a raucous crowd not to gang-rape two men he was sheltering as his guests. While begging them not to do it, he even forces his own two virgin daughters out of the house, so that the crowd of men could rape them instead! Although laws criminalizing "sodomy," still in effect in seventy-two nations, were repealed in the United States in 2003, these strong prohibitions reverberate into the present, especially for people who read them as if God dictated them in person.

Yet even those who have left these ancient traditions behind may experience the effects of such views, as I did. Even today, some traditionally minded Christians invoke teachings attributed to the apostle Paul, which picture Eve as gullible and sinful, and admonish women to be silent, subordinate, and to have babies:

> I do not allow any woman to teach or have authority over a man; she is to keep silent. For Adam was made first, then Eve; and Adam was not deceived, but the woman was deceived, and became a transgressor. Yet woman will be saved through bearing children, provided they remain faithful in love and holiness, with modesty.

Other Christians, like the African convert Tertullian, indicted their "sisters in Christ" as Eve's coconspirators:

> You are the devil's gateway . . . you are she who persuaded him who the devil did not dare attack. . . . Don't you know that every one of you is an Eve? The sentence of God on your sex lives on in this age; the guilt, of necessity, lives on too.

There's nothing particularly Christian about misogyny, of course—some Jewish and Buddhist sources say such things, as do passages in the Koran. Yet as we noted, women in such cultures, religious or not, often internalize such attitudes early, as I did, until the women's movement initiated a cultural exorcism, and the Nag Hammadi texts invited us to laugh, protest, or both. The Nag Hammadi sources show that even thousands of

years ago, some people were asking, "Why take that story literally, when doing so makes no sense?" Are we to believe that Adam
and Eve actually heard God's footsteps crunching leaves, when,
as *Genesis* says, "they heard the sound of the Lord God walking
in the garden in the cool of the day"? Was God lying when he
warned Adam and Eve that they would die *on the day* they ate
the forbidden fruit, since that didn't happen? And wasn't it the
snake who actually told them the truth? Why would God deny
humans knowledge that he admits could make them "like one of
us"—that is, like divine beings?

Not everyone who asked those questions dismissed the story
as nonsense; some read it as myth or allegory, inviting the spiritually adventurous to plunge into its hidden depths. The anonymous author of another Nag Hammadi text, titled the *Testimony
of Truth*, noting that the Lord acts like a vindictive tyrant, jealous of his human creatures, after asking "What kind of God is
this?" dares claim that the serpent, who seeks to liberate them,
"is Christ"! Others read the story symbolically, suggesting that
the story of Eve's emerging from Adam's body is meant to show
how our soul, or *psyche*, may come to recognize divine wisdom
hidden deep within us. Discovering these long-suppressed
sources invites us to uncover hidden continents of our own cultural landscape. And when we do, we gain perspective on reflexive attitudes that we may have unthinkingly inherited, just at a
time when countless people are exploring a much wider range of
gender identity, letting go of the assumption that gender difference, as our culture defines it, is built into our DNA.

After evangelical Christianity shattered the ceiling of the
constricted world I'd known before, the secret gospels opened
up a far larger universe. Having lived for too long in a world that

ignored or denigrated anything spiritual, I found that reading the story of Adam and Eve as showing how the human *psyche*, ignorant of spirit, may wake up, in pain and joy, to the presence of the spirit, spoke to my own experience—even before I knew that spiritual awakening was possible.

CHAPTER 3

A Lifetime

Elaine with Mark in New York, when he was three weeks old.

D o you have children?"

"No; we very much hope to have children, but it hasn't happened yet."

By the time my friend Mary Beth Edelson, an artist, asked me this question, Heinz and I had been married for seven years, hoping, then longing, for children. Finally we consulted a fertility specialist, although this field of medicine was in its early stages. Our Belgian physician prescribed intense doses of weekly hormone injections and blood tests, varying the medications and dosage for three years. Month after month, the treatments caused physical discomfort, along with repeated cycles of hope and disappointment, followed by another year and a half of daily injections and blood tests. When I told her this, Mary Beth said, "Let's do a ritual for you. I only did it once before, but it worked."

Surprised and embarrassed, I was also intrigued. Mary Beth lived in a large loft in downtown New York filled with her husband's sculptures, making art and creating rituals as performance art, in which she invited the audience to participate. Impressed by the "Ritual for an End to Bitterness," which she performed in the SoHo loft called the Kitchen, I asked, "How did you choose to do *that*?"

"I wanted to create a ritual to celebrate," she answered, "but discovered that what prevents many people from celebrating is bitterness; so I started with this one." Although I knew that fertility rituals have long been traditional in many cultures, the idea of participating in one felt strange, unless, perhaps, as art. But why not? After reflecting on her offer, and discussing it with Heinz, who found it amusing, I realized I had nothing to lose.

On a clear evening in February, feeling nervous, foolish, and excited, I arrived at Mary Beth's loft, along with the few friends we'd invited: Sharon, Lizzie, and Lizzie's partner, Emily, all of whom, like Mary Beth, had children; and Carolee Schneemann, an artist and filmmaker. Mary Beth initiated the evening by playing the sound of ocean waves breaking on a beach, as we sat quietly, focusing on a large diorama. As the evening darkened into night, she lit candles and asked me to sit inside a large, hollow sculpture, as each participant, in turn, spoke about giving birth. In that enclosed space, shaped almost like a birth canal, I felt the ritual focus intensify. Suddenly a single question formed in my mind: "Are you willing to be a channel?" That jolted me into awareness of something that had never entered my consciousness: I was terrified of dying in childbirth. In the shock of that recognition, something changed, perhaps an involuntary release of muscles tensed with fear. Later, astonished by what had happened, I couldn't recall ever hearing anyone talk about a woman dying in childbirth, often as it has happened in other times and places; instead, this felt like a genetic memory of countless women's experiences, stored in the cells of our bodies. During the final, intensely focused moments of our gathering, another sentence formed itself, startling me, as if speaking to my intense desire to control what we can't control: "You don't have to do this; it does itself."

Three weeks later, for the first time in my life, I discovered that I was pregnant. We were overjoyed, and the following October, on the clear and beautiful Sunday morning of the New York City Marathon, we drove to the hospital. Heinz stayed with me throughout the birth, encouraging Lamaze breathing; and although at moments the doctor was concerned about the baby, we were relieved, ecstatic, when our son Mark was born. Naive new parents, we marveled at him, finding him perfect. That afternoon, when a nurse took him to weigh him and do routine procedures, impatiently waiting for her to bring him back, I felt ferociously protective. Having previously experienced sexuality as the most powerful instinct, I now felt that this is what sexuality is *for*.

The next day, though, physicians at Babies Hospital, concerned about Mark's heartbeat, ordered an echocardiogram. I sat in the back of the room while they examined the images and engaged in intense discussion. I couldn't hear what they were saying, but caught the tone: something was wrong. When finally they called us into a conference room, they told us that Mark was born with a hole in one of the walls of his heart. Five years earlier, they said, a baby born with this condition invariably died. But since then, one of their pediatric cardiologists had invented an operation to make a repair, placing into the heart a plastic patch, over which tissue could grow. Since operating on a newborn is especially risky, they advised us to delay open-heart surgery until his first birthday.

Released from the hospital, we were hugely relieved to take Mark home and resume a semblance of normal life, while he slept in a tiny carrying crib next to our bed, where I often woke to check on him, breastfeeding, holding him close. A few weeks later, we were grateful to have the support of Jean Da Silva, a wonderfully experienced woman from England, who told me when we met, "I've been a nanny since I was eighteen." By this time, having married an American soldier, she had three children of her own. Her competence with babies hugely alleviated our concern for Mark's health, and we could see that she, too, came to love him dearly. More than two months later, Heinz and I went out for dinner together for the first time since his birth, but rushed home to be with him.

As that first anxiety eased, life with Mark seemed nearly normal; he smiled easily and was growing. After six months, he was sleeping in the baby's bedroom under a mobile of stars. That year flew by, with visits to his adoring grandmother at Thanksgiving and Christmas. And although we usually spent summers in the mountains of Colorado, where physicists gathered from all over the world to do physics and hike on mountain trails, that summer, careful not to take Mark to high altitude, we flew instead to California, where I could keep him close to me, and where Heinz could meet with physicists at Berkeley, Stanford, and Santa Cruz.

In Santa Cruz, we found a place we loved: a large one-room log cabin with a sleeping loft, nestled in a redwood forest that opened to a pasture where five Arabian horses grazed in a grassy meadow. That summer Mark often laughed with delight, especially when his father held him in his large hands, the two of them laughing together. On afternoon walks, I held our baby next to my breasts in a blue terry cloth carrier as we walked barefoot on the beach while the waves washed around our feet, stopping to pick up shells and disentangle seaweed from our ankles as we listened to the cry of the gulls and watched the pelicans. Mark was excited to learn to stand, first cruising around a low table, then holding on to my fingers with both hands, eager to walk to the meadow as the horses cantered to meet us at the fence, anticipating the carrots that we offered while stroking their long noses. Friends often stopped by at the cabin to sit and talk and drink iced tea during warm summer afternoons; indoors, with Mark next to me, or outside, holding him in the baby carrier, I loved to hear Heinz and his friend Nick, another physicist, talking and laughing.

Below days that might have looked idyllic, though, ran dark currents of terror. Each day brought us closer to Mark's October birthday—the day scheduled for open-heart surgery at Babies Hospital. Often, now, while preparing dinner in the evening, I began to drink more wine, welcome as an anesthetic to slightly mute the fear. I was careful never to drink more than one glass before dinner, another half glass during dinner, but I instinctively kept this secret, sensing that my capacity for alcohol was limited. Since I didn't slur words or get drunk, no one could possibly notice, or so I hoped. But one day Heinz let me know that he'd noticed, saying quietly, but firmly, "I love you, but I'm not going to watch you destroy yourself." Shocked and horrified that he'd noticed this secret, yet also relieved, I went to talk with a close friend.

The next day, shaking with shame and fear, I drove to a small church in Boulder Creek, walked down the concrete steps to the basement, and slipped into a metal chair in the back of a meeting of Alcoholics Anonymous. Even when others nodded at me, acknowledging a newcomer, I didn't speak; surely I didn't belong there—or did I? What the speaker told of repeated drunk driving, lost jobs, fighting with his family, and time in jail reassured me that I had nothing in common with him. But others spoke simply of wanting alcohol as an anesthetic, as I did. Then I heard something that struck me powerfully, since it felt undeniably true: willpower alone could not quell the craving for alcohol; nothing less than a spiritual experience could do that. Now I knew that I had to stop drinking alcohol altogether, and did. Instead, what I needed was in the books that packed my bookshelf and were piled on the floor in the tack house behind the cabin—what already had engaged me for years: seeking a spiritual dimension. I'd published my book on the Gnostic Gospels the previous year, intuitively knowing what I needed; now I had to *practice* the insights I'd recognized in them. Without that anesthetic, the fear clarified, naked and inescapable. Often overcome, raw and feeling desperate, I could only try to meditate, breathe deeply, and ask for help—from my husband, from close friends, from the stars and redwood forests, from God.

When we returned to New York in September, every day felt like a countdown to October 26. The day before, as we walked toward Babies Hospital holding Mark, to check in for surgery the next morning, I noted the motto over the door: "Healing Comes from the Most High." After we'd signed a pile of papers for admission and surgery, Heinz went to work, and I stayed; he'd return in the late afternoon. After hours of blood tests, heart monitors, blood pressure tests, physicians with clusters of young residents walking into a blank room with neon lights to look at Mark, somberly discussing the case as I held him, they finally left us alone, and he fell asleep in a hospital crib with iron bars. Since I refused to leave him by himself, even for a moment, I asked the nurses for a canvas sleeping cot. "Nothing available; besides, the hospital doesn't allow parents to stay overnight." When Heinz returned, he urged me to take a break from the hospital, while he walked the halls holding Mark, singing and talking.

Pushing open the hospital's heavy front door, relieved to step out of those arid halls, I hailed a taxi and headed downtown to the Lutheran church on Central Park West, where every Sunday afternoon during the church year the choir sings a Bach cantata. Sinking into a wooden pew in the back, I was grateful to hear the powerful, familiar words of the "Reformation" cantata: "A mighty fortress is our God, a bulwark never failing . . ." Later, after stopping at the apartment to pick up a warmer coat and a blanket, I went back to join my family, carrying sandwiches wrapped in plastic and milk in paper cartons. That evening we shared them in Mark's room, and stayed together until the head nurse sternly ordered us to leave: "Visiting hours are over." Since Heinz had to be at work the next day, he finally left to get some sleep. Despite the nurses' protests, I spread my coat and a blanket on the concrete floor, and prepared to spend the night next to Mark's crib. After several more doctors' rounds and nurses' checkups, quiet descended around midnight.

Anticipating surgery early the next morning, I could not sleep. Suddenly, after several hours stretched out on the cold floor while Mark slept, I sensed that I was not alone. Sitting up, I seemed to be sitting among women seated in a circle, holding hands. The only one I recognized was Nelle Morton, a revered and beloved older colleague, who'd retired from teaching at Drew University the year before and now lived in California. Surprised and comforted by the sense of their presence, I then realized, as in a lucid dream, that I could add people to the circle. I mentally added my parents and brother, also in California. During those moments, the ache of the hard floor drained away, along with anxiety and exhaustion, as a fresh rush of energy flowed into the room. How long it lasted I do not know, but it offered considerable reassurance; then they were gone, and I began to rest.

Hours later, around four in the morning, I was startled by something else that may have been a dream, although I didn't seem to be asleep. In that dream, or whatever it was, a menacing being, male but inhuman, approached me, smelling like danger, wordlessly threatening death—Mark's death. Terrified, I fought an impulse to turn and run, feeling that if I did, everything would be lost. Then I recalled something our dance teacher often had said: "Put weight in your feet, and stand." When I did, the dark figure retreated. But then he came toward us a second time, even more frightening. Again I longed to run, but resisted, and managed to stand against him. Once again he retreated, only to return a third time, more terrifying than ever. Feeling that I could not possibly stand a moment longer, I spoke a name: "Jesus Christ!" At that, the dangerous being fled, and my fear dissolved. Now I felt certain that the surgery would go well.

Later, shaken by that experience, I realized that, in extremity, terrified of losing our child in open-heart surgery, I'd called out a name I'd heard that afternoon during the singing: one stanza of Bach's cantata speaks of how "our ancient foe," the devil, "seeks to work us woe . . . on earth is not his equal." Then Bach's music builds chords suggesting triumph over harm and death: "one little word shall fell him." In the dream I'd spoken names of *Jesus*, which Christians have invoked for millennia as words with power to exorcise danger and death. While not imagining that I'd actually seen the devil, I'd instinctively reached for these words when fearing for our son's life.

Early that morning, Heinz arrived, and we held Mark close

as physicians injected him with a sedative, then strapped his small body onto a gurney and wheeled him away from us into the operating room. As we sat huddled together, holding hands, I told Heinz what I'd envisioned that night; the morning felt strangely peaceful. During those interminable hours of waiting, I sat down at a small table and wrote a note to Nelle Morton, telling her that I'd felt that she and other women somehow had been present with me the night before, in Mark's hospital room.

Finally one of the surgeons emerged to say that the surgery had gone well. They'd made the repair; now Mark was recovering in intensive care. We were allowed to go in and see him, caged in what looked like a glass incubator, but not to come close. Many hours later, when the staff finally allowed me in, his slight, thin body was pinned to a board in a dense complex of intravenous needles and monitoring cables. Ordered not to touch him, lest he risk infection, I softly spoke to him, so that he'd know I was there. Hearing my voice, he suddenly lurched his whole upper body toward me, ripping out the needles on one arm. At that, a nurse charged in, shouting, "Can't you see you're disturbing him? He's got to rest; you can't come in here!" Immediately I fled, shocked and weeping, blaming myself for having possibly harmed my child. I ran down the halls and dashed out into the street, heedless of traffic, feeling that I didn't care if I were struck by a car, maybe even deserved to be.

In retrospect, I began to sort out what had happened. In that terrible moment, I felt as if the nurse was right: I was guilty of causing Mark's fragile, nearly desperate, condition. Only much later did I realize the truth: *I'd rather feel guilty than helpless.* For guilt, however painful, often masks a deeper agony, even more unbearable. Standing there, seeing Mark in intensive care, a huge scar on his thin chest where the physicians had cut it open, broken his breastbone, and stopped his heart to repair it, we were utterly helpless—helpless to do anything at all about what mattered more than our own lives.

Slowly, during the days that followed, although the hospital staff would not yet let us touch or hold him, Mark began to take in nourishment, regain some strength. Finally the days and nights, previously indistinguishable, began to take shape again. By the fourth day, realizing that he was getting better, I finally allowed myself to sleep at home for several hours at a time. Heinz and I took turns staying at the hospital, sometimes asking Jean Da Silva to stay with him while we took a break. Stopping by the apartment to change clothes, I found a note from Nelle Morton, sent while my note was still on its way to her. She wrote to tell me that on the night before Mark's surgery, she and the women in her "sister circle" had met, sitting on the floor of her living room in California, to pray for us.

On the fifth day, while Mark was still in the hospital, a well-meaning older friend, noting my exhaustion, said, "Dear, you look like a professor; you've got to take care of yourself! If you didn't *have* to work, would you still teach?" Since she'd never had a profession, her question surprised me, and I said, "Of course not, not now!" That afternoon, when I went back to the apartment to take a shower and change clothes, Jean, who arrived carrying brown paper bags full of groceries, said, "You had a phone call; it sounded important." He'd called twice, "a Mr. MacArthur from some foundation. He said please call him back right away." Before leaving for the hospital, I returned the call. Answering, he said, "Congratulations"—for what? He identified himself as Rod MacArthur, calling in person to tell me that I'd received a fellowship from his foundation. "How can that be, since I haven't applied for any?" He explained that no one can apply for what outsiders call the "genius grant"; instead, recipients are nominated without their knowledge, on the basis of their creative work. Now I recalled that I'd heard something about these; that, as he explained, the foundation offered five years of complete support—no applications, no requirements, no reports, no questions asked. Stunned, I called Heinz, who asked, "Is this a joke? Is this true?" I dived into a taxi and went back to the hospital to be with Mark. The following morning, Heinz called to tell me that a press release had announced the award in the *New York Times*.

On the tenth day after surgery, the physicians allowed us to sign Mark out of the hospital and carry him home, wrapped in his favorite blanket. Although thin and pale, his skin almost translucent, he beamed with delight to be back. Heinz stretched out on the living room floor with him as they began to build New York City out of bright cardboard bricks, and to put down wooden tracks for a set of trains. One day, shortly after he came home, while I was holding him in the rocking chair and singing, as I often did, his usual curious and happy equilibrium shattered. He loved our songs, but when I began to sing "Ezekiel saw the wheel / Way up in the middle of the air," he suddenly looked at the ceiling, terrified. Immediately I felt I knew what it was— the bright circles of light on the ceiling of the operating room— and guessed that during those long hours of surgery, there may have been moments when, to some extent, the anesthesia had worn off, when he may have seen lights like that. I never sang that song to him again, and the episode passed.

Our lives began to resume their normal rhythm, far easier now that the surgery was behind us; and the MacArthur Fellowship, like a miracle, offered what now I longed for most: time. As a beginning assistant professor at Barnard, besides teaching full time, I'd had to take on administrative work, writing budgets and reports as acting chair for our tiny department. The dean and the president of Barnard, astonished that one of their untenured, virtually unknown faculty members had received such an honor, called me into the dean's office to congratulate me. "What do you want from us," they asked, "since they're offering to pay your full salary for five years?" "Time to be home with our son," I replied, "and to think and write, in an office without a phone!"

After the controversy that followed the publication of *The Gnostic Gospels*, the grant came not only as a gift of time and energy, but also as an enormous vote of confidence. Hugely grateful, I was able to be with Mark as he grew strong again; the doctors were pleased that the heart repair had succeeded. Whenever I could find a spare hour while Jean was with us, I went to a tiny maid's room in the concrete basement of a friends' apartment building that served as my study to read and write. But just as my book on the Gnostic gospel was receiving recognition that surprised us both, Heinz was dealing with an unexpected setback. Before he'd arrived in New York, he'd received two offers of faculty positions: one at Columbia, the other at Rockefeller University. He chose Rockefeller, especially since the senior physicist who chaired the department enthusiastically promised to support his promotion to tenure. When the time came, though, other colleagues told Heinz that the chairman had broken his promise. Hearing what happened, I was

distressed to see him so upset, and concerned that the dispar-
ity between our careers at that moment might divide us. When
we talked about it at length, I anxiously tried to suggest what I
thought might help, until he said simply, "You can't solve this,
and you don't have to try: I just need you to listen." Publicly, he
dealt with professional disappointment with equanimity that
earned his colleagues' respect; privately, I was moved by his
grace under pressure.

That spring, though, we had a marital head-on collision.
When we took Mark to his pediatric cardiologist for a checkup,
she asked, "What are your plans for the summer?" Excited, we
told her that we were going to Colorado, where physicists met
from all over the world at the Center for Physics, a series of simple wooden offices, shaded with aspens and pines, within sight
of the high mountains. We were eager to return to what felt like
a normal life in Colorado, where we'd often hiked on Saturdays,
walking up dirt trails through forests of aspen and pine, up to
boulder fields and high mountain lakes, sometimes camping
out, sleeping bags unrolled by a campfire, watching the brilliant
stars until we fell asleep. During the week, when the physicists
weren't writing equations on a blackboard or standing around
the coffee maker talking about particles and galaxies, they were
often bicycling up mountain roads or planning the next hike up
some mountain pass, walking through snow patches among the
wildflowers.

Hearing this, Mark's doctor said nothing. Then she told us
to come back the following week, and ordered her colleagues to
meet with us. As we sat in one of the identical green consulting rooms at the hospital, the doctors' message was clear: "We
strongly advise you not to take this child to high altitude. Right

now he's doing fine. But you need to know that there is a slight chance that in his condition, he might develop pulmonary hypertension—a lung disease, invariably fatal—if exposed to the stress of breathing at high altitude." "What are you calling a 'slight chance'?" Heinz asked. "About one in ten thousand."

When we walked outside, shocked, and drove downtown, at first we were silent. Then Heinz said, "One chance in ten thousand? That's ridiculous—more likely we'd be run over by a truck." As we talked it over later, we could not agree. "If there's *any* chance that something we do could cause him harm, we can't take that chance," I said, "or, at least, *I* can't." At first I assumed that he was simply being stubborn about what he wanted to do, despite the risk; he insisted I was overcautious. As we struggled through these conversations, I began to see that he could not bear to imagine that our son really could be at risk again, so deeply did he long to believe that Mark was well. After three weeks of painful conflict, we resolved it: Mark and I would fly to California and meet friends there, while Heinz would go to Colorado for two weeks, then join us in the cabin in the redwoods for the rest of the summer.

Returning to the Santa Cruz mountains in California, Mark and I breathed in the smell of the woods, and the horses ran to greet us. This time we'd brought along Mark's African gray parrot, and discovered that he loved to sit outside in the apple tree in front of the cabin, conversing with the local birds; then he'd hop onto our shoulders as we carried him back inside. When Heinz arrived, we drove to the ocean every afternoon. Even when the weather was cold and windy, father and son would dig in the sand, building sandcastles with moats and walls, until we'd shake off the sand and drive back to the cabin to make dinner. There we'd set a fire in the fireplace to talk and tell stories until it got dark, then climb up to the sleeping loft and fall asleep, listening to the counterpoint percussion of the frogs and crickets. On sunnier days, we'd walk to the boardwalk for popcorn or cotton candy, to ride on the merry-go-round, the bumper cars, and the Ferris wheel. For a couple of hours each morning, Rebekah Edwards, a quiet, generous young writer whom Mark loved, would come to spend time with him while Heinz sat at the table in the cabin doing physics. Behind the cabin, in the tack house, the walls hung with saddles and bridles, I would read and write during those morning hours, at a table I'd set up looking at the creek outside the window.

One evening, when a friend came to dinner at the cabin, he turned the conversation to ask when children start to talk. I turned to Mark, then one and a half, and asked, "Mark, why don't you talk yet?" As we expected, he said nothing. But later that evening, while I was giving him a bath, and he was maneuvering plastic boats and small floating dinosaurs, he suddenly stopped, looked at me, and said, "I don't want to talk yet." Astonished, since I'd never heard him speak a complete sentence, I burst out laughing, then sang him a song from the *Mikado*, about a bird that didn't want to talk; then said, "Well then, Mark, just talk when you're ready." When I told Heinz about it, he said that he himself had hardly spoken at all until he was three, since he'd been so fascinated with what was going on in his mind that he felt that putting it into words would mean cramming far too much into inadequate vessels. Mark's mind, like his, was far less verbal than visual and spatial.

Back in New York, Mark loved our excursions to Central Park, where we met other children in the playground, digging in the sand, running to the swings, and climbing the slides, watching the squirrels and dogs. Mark and I claimed as "our tree" a stout oak tree in Central Park with branches that we could climb together. Sitting among the leaves and talking, or arranging the rocks below to make paths, we spent countless hours in our secret garden, our outdoor "house." But that spring, when he was two and a half, he surprised me by asking, "Where's my school?" *Your school—you're only two!* I thought. Startled, I wondered how he had realized, while I hadn't, that next fall the park would be empty of children his age, since they'd all be in nursery school. So after scrambling to find out about such schools, we finally found one upstairs in the Park Avenue Methodist Church. There, in the fall, he met Bram, who became his best friend—his best *child* friend, he told me, since Rebekah, in California, was his best *grown-up* friend. Every morning he eagerly anticipated going to his "school," which initiated a round of children's birthday parties, Halloween, Thanksgiving, and Christmas at his grandmother's house, which brought a new red tricycle. Although Mark was always thin, his chest marked by the surgical scar, he was active and curious, and loved riding his tricycle on the paths through the park, or riding on Heinz's shoulders during our weekend adventures in New York.

That spring, his cardiologist, who routinely checked the results of the surgery, ordered a cardiac catheterization, about a one-hour procedure. After we checked into Babies Hospital, they injected a sedative and wheeled him away, while we sat in the waiting room. After one hour passed, then two, then *four*, someone emerged to tell us that they'd had to repeat the procedure, since they'd gotten a false result. That day felt endless, wearing us down with worry and exhaustion. In the evening, *nine hours* after they started, several doctors emerged, without speaking, and a nurse summoned us to sit down with them in a conference room. "We couldn't believe it," they said. "We thought the result must be wrong. We kept doing it over and over, hoping for a different result. The surgical repair was fine; we thought he was well; but we keep getting the same result. Your son has a very rare disease: pulmonary hypertension, invariably fatal."

We sat silent, in shock. Finally we asked, "What does that mean? What do you recommend?"

"We're sorry. There's no treatment, no cure. Short of a heart-lung transplant, that is—now only in experimental stages, medically inadvisable, especially for a child."

Invariably fatal. I remember nothing else that was said, until finally I asked, "How long?"

"We don't know; a few months, maybe a few years."

The following day, a team of doctors urged us to authorize a lung biopsy. They explained that they'd take a slice of the lung, which would require another incision: "Here are the papers; just sign these to give your permission."

"How could that help?" I asked.

"It can't help with the prognosis," they said, "but the procedure will show us how far the disease has progressed."

Mark was already starkly pale, exhausted from the previous day's ordeal. Holding him, I felt certain that if more masked strangers poked needles and knives into him in an operating room, he might lose heart—literally—and die. Were the physicians now seeing him as an experimental subject to be opened up so that they might gather statistics for research papers they would publish in the *New England Journal of Medicine*? "No," I said; "we're going home." We refused to sign, gathered Peter Rabbit and Mark's blanket, and carried him home.

We resumed what looked like normal life, in a universe irrevocably changed. Mark regained his energy, eagerly returning to school, where he and his best friend, Bram, invented elaborate games involving ongoing stories known only to the two of them, building tunnels and cities with blocks, climbing in the playground on the roof. In another year punctuated with children's birthday parties, Mark was excited to begin karate, learning to stand, kick, and fight. These lessons engaged him with his favorite program on television—an animated cartoon series featuring the young Prince Adam, who, in crisis, turned into the mighty fighter He-Man, Master of the Universe. Like his older cousin Superman, He-Man managed astonishing feats to rescue people from Skeletor, the evil villain who sought to dominate and destroy the whole world. Watching with him, I wondered, Did these television writers raid Gnostic mythology to create these characters, or did they spontaneously reinvent them? Mark reveled in these stories, seeing himself living in them, as I'd lived in Oz, and as evangelical Christians I'd known saw themselves contending with the power of God and Satan. Once, standing on a redwood stump in California, Mark struck a karate pose, and told me, "I came here to fight"—understanding, I felt, that he was, indeed, fighting against death for the vivid flame of his young life.

More grateful than ever to the MacArthur Foundation, I was able to spend that time with him; for soon, when he was three and a half, we made the rounds of "interviews" for kindergarten, during which school administrators at various New York schools seemed intent on assessing each three-year-old's chances of getting into a college like Harvard. *That's* not *what matters to us,* I thought. *We've been there, done that. Besides, this child may never go to college. Where can he best thrive now?* Since his pediatrician knew the local schools, and was on call for several of them, he agreed with our decision not to tell them of Mark's condition, lest they treat him like a china doll (I avoided saying, even to myself, "like a dying child," since I fiercely refused to accept that diagnosis). Much later, though, I realized how that secret isolated us from other parents, even from the parents of his friends at school. Mercifully, his illness was invisible. Except for being thin, he looked and acted like other children, and since no treatment could help, he was spared medical ordeals.

One sunny afternoon, as he was riding his red tricycle through Central Park, he declared that the Town School, which we'd visited, was "my school"—a place filled with sunlight, with views of the East River, where Mr. Brockman, a large, huggable, bearlike kindergarten teacher, had set up a woodworking shop in the back of his classroom. We didn't tell Mark that he hadn't been admitted and was only on the waiting list; but when it cleared, the classroom at the Town School with Joshua Brockman, whom he adored, became his school.

Meanwhile, physicians at Babies Hospital who knew me because of Mark's diagnosis asked me to join the bioethics committee for the neonatal intensive care unit—not the ordinary one, but a separate one reserved for babies and children born with serious, usually terminal, illnesses. At each meeting, physicians would present cases that involved disputed decisions about appropriate care: the baby who had been kept alive for weeks on a heart-lung machine, ordinarily used only for a few hours at a time during open-heart surgery; the Siamese twins from Colombia, only one of whom, the physicians explained, could survive the surgery necessary to separate them; the infants born to addicts, already addicted to crack cocaine themselves; the two-year-old whose parents refused surgery for religious reasons. As a medical outsider, and especially as Mark's mother, hearing these intense discussions gradually helped me face the wholly unacceptable fact that there are many situations that medicine can't cure. Most often, in the cases we heard, the physicians, nurses, and staff, hardworking and conscientious as I knew them to be, could do nothing. I noted, too, the staff pediatrician who, when her seven-year-old daughter was diagnosed with inoperable cancer, took her child home to die, rather than subject her to medical torture to prolong her life.

After each of these meetings, I felt exhausted walking back through the intensive care unit. Intensive care is a godsend when it can keep someone alive through a crisis; here, though, it served mainly to stretch out each child's dying for weeks, even for months and years. Physicians dealing with children seemed to feel that they had to try everything to keep a child alive as long as possible, even under the most extreme conditions. So when my term on the committee ended, the medical staff, knowing of Mark's condition, were surprised by what I said when thanking them for the opportunity to work with them. "I have great admiration for what you do, and what you deal with every day," I said. "But what you call 'heroic measures' are often superheroic measures. For the sake of the children, please consider stopping earlier than you usually do." And every time I left the hospital after one of those painful meetings, I would breathe with gratitude that Mark was in school, climbing, building, practicing letters, in sunlit classrooms at the Town School.

At the same time, contending with his dreadful diagnosis, I asked Mark's godfather, an analytic psychiatrist, to refer me to a colleague with whom I could talk freely, to avoid inflicting emotional storms on Mark or Heinz. While talking with the compassionate, incisive man he recommended, I struggled hard with my own powerlessness, which spurred an intense interest in magic. I felt I'd give anything to know how to do it, whatever it took—a spell, a cure, a bargain with invisible powers. How could we go on living, having no control over what mattered more than our own lives?

Every morning that year looked gray when I woke up; sometimes lighter gray during the morning hours, darker in the afternoon. The psychiatrist called it "situational depression," since I'd never suffered from depression before; now grief mixed with guilt and isolation. I knew no one whose child had died, and I learned only much later that it happens far more often than I'd ever imagined; even the ancients, who so often experienced the death of their children, called it "the unbearable grief." When one day my empathetic psychiatrist suggested "Why not regard your students as your children?" I was stunned into silence, then stammered, "I'm not *that* crazy." How neurotic would *that* be, for them and for me? Had I never had children, I might have been able to hear what he suggested, but now, as Mark's mother, I knew that only caring for children could possibly matter, confronting such a loss.

Ever since Mark's cardiologist presided at the diagnosis, she'd urged me to talk with one of the nurses at Babies Hospital. For over a year I adamantly refused, since I knew that she

was the nurse to whom they referred parents of dying children—
and privately, I'd sworn that *our son is not going to die.* But after
fighting huge resistance for a year and a half, I finally called the
nurses' office to make an appointment. When I arrived at Babies
Hospital, after slowly finding my way to her office, her secretary
said she'd been expecting me. After closing the door behind me,
she asked me to sit down, and said simply, "There's a name for
what you are going through: it's called 'mourning.' That doesn't
start when someone dies; it starts with the diagnosis." Much as
I hated hearing it, as my body sank into desolation, I registered
what she said. It was years before I could acknowledge that her
words also brought some relief, perhaps some slight measure of
acceptance of something I'd sought so long to deny.

When we returned to California for the summer, I was torn
apart. Believing what the doctors told us, I felt, would amount to
betraying Mark, might hint that we were giving up on him, but
denying what they said had solved nothing. At the same time, denying the diagnosis was not a choice; it was simply what we did.
Since we were fighting for Mark's life along with him, we decided
to consult other doctors as well. First we made appointments at
Massachusetts General, and spent two days meeting with several teams of specialists there. Later, we flew with Mark to San
Francisco, to consult a pediatric pulmonologist famous for his
work with this disease; but he, too, slowly, kindly told us that he
agreed with the others: no treatment, no cure.

Back in California for the summer, I no longer had the
slight anesthetic of wine to ease an agony deeper than anything I'd ever imagined. Having sometimes smoked cigarettes
in graduate school, I began to smoke again, almost purpose-
fully. Heinz disliked smoking, having quit years earlier, and I

disliked it as well, but I defended myself inwardly, thinking, *Don't I have a perfectly good reason to do anything at all that might ease the stress?* At the same time, I kept asking, *Why am I doing this?* At first I thought that I was trying to take on Mark's illness and transfer the lung disease from him to me. Magical thinking; but for a moment it made me feel justified, or perhaps suitably punished, for not being able to protect him. But early July brought a sudden shock of recognition. Could it be that I was trying to kill myself? Suicide was not an option I'd ever considered, but since I could not imagine seeing him die, was I somehow choosing to bring a lung disease on myself, so that I wouldn't have to live through his illness, possibly even through his death? Horrified, I thought, What if I succeeded? How would that affect Mark and Heinz? How could they deal with what Mark needed, if they had to deal with my death as well? That question struck like lightning; and the moment it did, I immediately quit smoking, never to touch it again. That happened on July fourth—a new kind of Independence Day— once I'd faced down a fraction of the fear.

When we returned to New York, I imagined that Mark would regret leaving the California woods, forests, and ocean, as I did; but instead, he gleefully shouted, "Back home!" Now I resolved to treasure every day, making sure to buy our favorite groceries for dinner, often stopping to buy a helium balloon to bring home for him. After I brought him new crayons with a large sketchpad, he proudly presented me with his "first book." On page one, he drew a heart—not a Valentine's heart, but a child's version of an anatomical drawing—and told me what to write below it: "This is a heart, beating." I was amazed; how clearly he knew what mattered. He eagerly explained that he was planning a television show that he would call "Worlds of Wonder," about bees, water, dinosaurs, dragonflies, stars, and the sun. And every night, Heinz regaled him with stories he made up about various tribes of dragons—the striped dragons, the polka-dot dragons, and other dragon species, in ongoing sagas the two of them shared. One morning in New York, as Mark and I sat together on a low, leafy branch of "our tree" in Central Park, he confided, "I'm the king of the dragons. And the queen of the dragons is named Sarah." "Who do you know named Sarah?" I asked, expecting that it would be someone in his class at school. "No one," he said.

Heinz and I fervently hoped for more children, but after a miscarriage, we began to talk with Hugh Hildesley, a priest at the Church of the Heavenly Rest in New York, about adopting a child. He told us of the Gladney Center for Adoption, an agency in Texas that people in the Presbyterian church had founded over a hundred years ago, to locate good homes for children whose birth parents were unable to care for them. Instead of accepting applications, which would have required more staff than the agency had, the staff would consider applications only from couples recommended by people they knew. Furthermore, the agency's staff worked hard to make the difficult situation of unexpected pregnancy as positive as possible for the birth mothers, most of them girls in high school. They could live there in dormitory rooms that looked like a college campus, where they could find support, understanding, and counseling, and take some classes. Since Hugh and other friends offered to recommend us, the agency agreed to consider us, and we flew down to Fort Worth. There we sat in a meeting with about forty other couples, where each of six birth mothers spoke to us, in turn, of her experience there, and why she had chosen to consider adoption at Gladney. My husband, who, like other scientists we knew, usually regarded church people as naive do-gooders, was impressed, and said, "This is what all those Christians *ought* to be doing!" So we began the arduous process of filling out dozens of forms, writing essays, making appointments for interviews, and assembling a large dossier of letters of recommendation, grateful that the agency finally put us on the list.

At the end of May we got the call that we'd been waiting for: Patti, the social worker we'd come to know well by now, invited us to come to meet the baby girl, just born, who their counselors felt could match our family. Excited, we immediately flew down to Fort Worth. When we first saw her, the pediatrician explained that she had been born over two months prematurely, and he would not allow us to bring her home until after her due date. I wept inconsolably when we left the agency for the Dallas airport: now we'd have to wait.

Back to the cabin in California, to the horses, the meadows, the ocean. One night, after dinner, Mark told me he'd dreamed that we were going to leave him in the cemetery that we drove past every day on our way to the ocean. Clearly he knew that he was vulnerable; a red scar ran down his chest where the surgeons had broken his sternum to operate during open-heart surgery. Heinz and I had agreed that we'd answer whatever questions he might ask as directly as possible, but not to initiate talk about dying. So when he told me about his dream, I froze, but struggled hard to listen. As he told me about it, we made a drawing of it together; he drew the grass, gravestones, and crosses, one with a stone angel on top.

Talking with him about his dream, I felt especially apprehensive about having initiated the adoption. Even though we wanted two children, was that an act of disloyalty to the son we adored? Could it suggest that we'd given up on Mark's life and were preparing for life without him? The three of us held each other especially close that summer, spending hours in the tree house in the redwoods, and, in the afternoons, wandering by the ocean, marveling at the sea anemone, the tiny crabs and sea snails in the tide pools. Mark was thinner than ever, but I tried not to notice, and mostly succeeded. Days before we were leaving California, his gray parrot, who every summer for three years had gloried in sitting in the apple tree each morning, flew away. Mark was devastated. Although we looked and called for him all afternoon until long after dark, we did not find him.

Just when we arrived back in New York, the call came: now we could bring our daughter home! When the three of us arrived in Fort Worth, carrying a bag packed with baby clothes and blankets, Patti ushered us into a room decorated with baby chicks and bunnies, and invited Mark to go with her, and be the first to see his new sister. After what felt like hours, Mark returned, smiling and proud as a big brother, helping Patti carry his new baby sister in a tiny carrier. As we marveled at meeting her, Patti asked, "What are you going to name her?" We'd already decided on a name, but seeing her, and realizing that she was nearly two and a half months old, we suddenly thought of what huge changes this tiny child would experience. Since she was leaving everything familiar to her, we felt it would be wrong to add any more changes that we could avoid. So I said, "You must already have a name for her; what do you call her?" Surprised, Patti replied, "We call her Sarah." Heinz and I looked at each other and nodded; we liked the name. "She must be used to her name: Sarah." In the excitement of that moment, I'd completely forgotten what Mark had said over a year before. Several years later, I found a journal in which I'd written it down. So one night when Sarah, then five years old, confessed to me her worry that, being adopted, she didn't really belong, I was able to tell her the story that reassures her that she belongs in our family; that even before she was born, her older brother, seeing her as "queen of the dragons," knew she was coming.

In September, Mark was eager to go back to school, where, with Mr. Brockman and his classmates, he was building a six-foot wooden airplane in the woodworking shop in back of the kindergarten class. In October, we had to postpone his birthday party, since he wasn't feeling well; but he recovered well enough to go out with us on weekend family adventures—most often to the Museum of Natural History, to see the dinosaurs, the giant squid, the jewels, and the planetarium's dazzling skies. On other days, we visited Mark's favorite place, the Air and Space Museum on the USS *Intrepid*, Heinz and Mark often walking ahead, holding hands, while I carried Sarah in a baby pack.

Two days before Christmas, Mark said he was hungry, and asked me to make a hamburger for him; but when I did, he felt too sick to eat, so we called the pediatrician for an appointment. This time Heinz took him. When they returned, Heinz's face was ashen. He signaled that we urgently needed to talk; and since Jean Da Silva was there to care for the children, we left together and drove downtown. He told me what our pediatrician had said: "You should be prepared for a sudden demise. But don't tell your wife." Seeing the center of Park Avenue brilliant with thousands of crystal Christmas lights, blurred with floods of tears, I felt every one of their points stabbing like needles.

Still, we breathed more easily in the New Year. Mark loved school; Sarah was growing, laughing, babbling in her own language, scooting across the expanse of oriental carpet, grabbing Mark's toys, which sometimes he tolerated, and sometimes didn't, the two of them playing and squabbling like inseparable siblings. But one night Mark told us that he wanted to call his beloved Rebekah, who lived in California. When we reached her, he pleaded with her to come to New York to visit us, soon. When she, living as a graduate student in San Francisco, explained that she couldn't afford the trip, he said, "You can have my money," offering her his savings account. Hearing this, we immediately sent her airline tickets, and she came; by then she, too, belonged to our extended family.

Late on a Wednesday afternoon in April, when I called the owner of the cabin in California to arrange for our summer's stay, he explained that it wasn't available, since his daughter was planning to be married there in June. We couldn't bear to tell that to Mark, so we decided to do so only after we'd found another place nearby. That evening, after Heinz told Mark his bedtime stories about the dragons, I went in to sing to him until he fell asleep. Instead, this time he clung to me, arms around my neck, and said, "I'll love you all my life, and all my death." Stunned, I stayed with him until he went to sleep, then walked into the living room. When finally I could speak, I told Heinz. Shocked as I was, he exclaimed, "He *couldn't* have said that." "*I couldn't have made it up.*" We sat close, holding each other, shaking with sobs, silently, so they couldn't be heard.

The next day, Mark did not feel like eating, but was eager to go to school. That afternoon, after bringing him home, I called his cardiologist to set up an appointment for the next morning. When we arrived at her hospital office, her secretary told us that she'd ordered routine tests to be done first. When the nurse came in to draw blood, I was holding Mark on my lap; after she inserted the needle and left the room, he stiffened, and his eyes rolled up. I ran down the hospital hall holding him in my arms, calling for help. Within two or three agonizingly long minutes, six or seven physicians converged in a treatment room, placed Mark on a table, and worked to revive him while I stood over him, holding him close, and speaking to him in a steady, reassuring voice. But at a certain moment I sensed that his life left his body, and the intimate connection we'd been sharing suddenly seemed to break. Moments later, when his cardiologist arrived, I turned toward her and fell down, losing consciousness. Then I seemed to be in a brilliant place, vividly green, with golden light.

When I came to, I was in another room down the hall, as a doctor revived me with smelling salts, and opened my eyes to see Heinz arriving in great haste. When he cried out, "Oh, it's over, it's over . . ." I said, "It's not over until it's over—let's ask him to come back and go to California with us." At that moment I somehow felt that Mark could hear us; I felt his presence near the ceiling of the room. Heinz and I sat together, clasped tightly, and spoke to him. Moments later, his cardiologist came in, saying, "I don't want to get your hopes up, but his heart had stopped, and now it's beating again." Immediately we went to the room where he was and held him; but he did not regain consciousness; shortly after that, the heartbeats stopped.

We don't know, of course, what happened. I had the clear

impression that he'd heard us and had gone back into his body, but found that it couldn't sustain his life, since oxygen could not circulate through his spent lungs. Strangely, I also sensed that he'd felt a burst of joy and relief to leave his exhausted body. Before that moment, I'd taken for granted what I'd learned, that death was the end, any thought of surviving death only fantasy. Although that may be true, what I experienced that day challenged that assumption. I was astonished, seeming to sense that Mark was all right, wherever he was, and that he was *somewhere*. But that didn't change what we felt: utter desolation.

We stayed in the same room long after his life departed. During those six or seven hours, his body and features changed, as death took them over. Finally we could see that he was completely gone, his body deserted. After midnight, Heinz gently put his arms around me and said, "It's time to go home," and I realized that there was nothing more to do. He was right, and we walked out of the room, down the corridor, and out the back door of the hospital. Mark's godparents had joined us at the hospital, and Sharon came back to the apartment, where Jean had stayed with Sarah. Later Sharon told me that around four A.M., when Sarah woke, she'd gotten up to care for her, but saw that, having heard the baby cry, I already was up, holding and feeding her in a rocking chair. Of this I remember nothing.

At the service for Mark, friends came from all parts of our lives, close friends and those we hadn't seen for years. I was amazed and grateful to see them, although I felt strange, as though we were walking naked in public, utterly defenseless, the bereaved parents touching the small plain wooden coffin, covered with a beautifully embroidered altar cloth. Close friends offered to play music, especially welcome, since words were impossible to absorb. Finally, "Amazing Grace," a song Mark loved, as Heinz and I walked out behind his coffin. We stood at the back of the church, weeping and hugging our friends, grateful to see godmother Sharon holding Sarah, now nine months old. Standing there, I seemed to see the whole scene embraced by a huge net made of ropes, with enormous spaces between the knots, through which we could be swept away at any moment, out of the world. I did not want to die, but desperately wanted to be anywhere but there; the pain was unbearable. Yet in that vision, or whatever it was, I felt that the intertwined knots were the connections with the people we loved, and that nothing else could have kept us in this world. The only words I remember from those moments was someone saying, "It's as though you were a channel"—words that startled me, recalling words from the ritual in which I'd participated before Mark was conceived. Much later, back at the apartment after the service, I heard Heinz say to Lizzie, "I would've given my life for him, but no one would take it."

Later, when we returned to the hospital to pick up Mark's blanket and clothes, his cardiologist stopped us, put her arms around us, and said, "I'm so sorry. If I'd seen him that day, I would have immediately put him into intensive care." She knew, of course, that he could not survive, and she wanted to let us down slowly—but at what cost of unimaginable suffering to Mark? Without a moment's hesitation, I turned to look into her eyes, and said, "Then thank God you didn't see him."

Times of mourning displace us from ordinary life. Sometime later, Rebekah, Mark's "best grown-up friend," told us that although she hadn't known of his death at the time, of course, on the day that Mark died, she'd been walking down the street in

San Francisco when she suddenly felt that he was walking with her, holding her hand, for just a few moments. Then, too, the physician who was the mother of Mark's "best child friend," and who, like the other parents at his school, knew nothing of Mark's lung disease, told us that on that same afternoon, her son Bram, also six years old, suddenly had a collapsed lung, and had been rushed to the hospital. Fortunately, that emergency was quickly resolved. Years later, I met Bram on a street in New York, walking with his mother, his wife, and their beautiful son, nearly two years old, in a stroller. Bram told me that he's now an emergency room physician, and his wife a pediatric oncologist.

Although we'd heard that many couples separate after the death of a child, Heinz and I drew even closer, and closer with Sarah. Heartbreak had opened up his heart to an enormous empathy. We were surprised, too, to admit to each other that in our devastation, we also felt some relief from the tension that had held us for years; the sword we'd felt hanging over our lives had fallen; what we'd most dreaded had happened.

Only years later did I realize that we'd barely escaped what I can only call a vision of hell. Had we ignored the risks when Mark was two and taken him to the mountains instead of to California, the doctors would have blamed *us* for putting his life in danger when they discovered pulmonary hypertension, saying—or thinking—"You should never have done it; we warned you!" Far worse, we would have blamed ourselves, and, likely, each other as well. In that case, our marriage, which sustained us, likely would not have survived. As it was, we were together and present, to support him and each other. Now we still had each other, our daughter, and the astonishing grace of the life that Mark had shared with us.

Recalling this now, I can tell only the husk of the story—a story known inwardly only by those who have experienced such a loss, which we'd wish for no one else to suffer. Those who have not often say, "I can't imagine how you felt, what that was like." I can hardly imagine it either, even having lived through it. Recently, when someone said that, I found myself answering, "Like being burned alive."

CHAPTER 4

Going On

Mark Pagels at kindergarten, the Town School, New York.

Two months after Mark died, friends of Heinz invited us to a festive dinner dance to celebrate their wedding anniversary. I was startled: "Dance? Now? Do they know what just happened?" They did, of course. After talking, we finally agreed. "Why not? We love to dance." So on the appointed evening, after hesitating about what to wear, I chose a flared blue silk dress, and clung to Heinz's hand as we entered the ballroom. Our hosts had seated us at their table, along with several other couples whom we didn't know. When the music started, we immediately stood up to dance; we hadn't danced in far too long. As tension began to release, we leaned into the music, weaving into movement and touch. No one spoke to us of what had happened, but I was surprised and moved to sense that some of them surely knew. On the dance floor, they surrounded us with unspoken care, acting on some protective instinct, like elephants who nudge the wounded into the center of the herd so that instead of falling behind, they keep moving along with the others.

Earlier that week, when Lizzie asked Heinz how he was doing, he deflected the question, saying, "Oh, I was just feeling sorry for myself." She was impressed with what she saw as his lack of self-pity, but I was concerned about the way he held his feelings close. The grief cut so deeply that he sometimes seemed distant, in shock. I began to see how chasms could open up between parents after a child's death, as so often they do: we longed to escape the river of grief we could see reflected in each other's eyes. Since we could barely talk about what happened—still too raw—we drew each other close by making love, stoking fires that, for moments at least, seemed to shut out death.

Until that spring, we'd expected to take Mark and Sarah,

now nine months old, to California for the summer, but now everything had changed. Instead of California, where we'd gone to protect Mark from high altitude, we'd go back to the Colorado mountains. First, though, we flew to California. Since no one in my family had come to Mark's funeral, my parents having excused themselves by saying that the trip was too stressful, I'd had a videotape made so that they could share it, too. When we visited months later, my mother was horrified when I suggested that she watch that video with me. Surprised and disappointed, I never dared mention it to my father or my brother. The atmosphere in their house felt stifling, surreal; no one mentioned Mark; apparently, he'd simply vanished. How had I managed to forget that our family's only response to death was stark and silent denial?

Now I recalled what had happened long ago when one of my high school friends came to live with our family for several weeks during our senior year, while her mother was hospitalized during surgery for breast cancer. I'd never imagined that her mother would die, since no one in my family had even hinted at that possibility. When she succumbed to that disease in her early forties, I went to her funeral, weeping as if inconsolable. I was shocked when her family invited me to join them afterward for a gathering where everyone ate, drank, talked, and hugged. I fled, confused and angry at what felt like their callousness: Shouldn't they all have gone home feeling desolate, to cry alone in a closet, as I did?

My father had fashioned his own escape from the turmoil of his family by putting aside emotion—and, with it, religion, so much driven by emotion. When he spoke of his parents, as he almost never did, he scowled, suggesting that they waged religious war in the household, wielding Calvinist dogma like hatchets, threatening fires of eternal damnation. While I was glad that he'd

bushwhacked his way out of whatever dark wilderness they inhabited, his choices had left us a meager emotional stew. Since our
parents treated anger, grief, and death as if they were insoluble,
we could do nothing but ignore them. Only decades later, when I
heard the anthropologist Clifford Geertz speak about what looked
like wildly bizarre practices—cremation rituals in Bali—did I hear
him speak of a path toward consolation: that "the work of culture
is to make suffering sufferable." So when my friend's relatives
gathered for a wake after her mother's funeral to eat, drink, and
talk, they understood far more than I'd ever imagined.

So besides the simple and powerful ritual we'd shared, heartbroken, at the Church of the Heavenly Rest, I needed to create another ritual of our own. After we left my parents' house to drive
back to the cabin in California where we had spent summers
with Mark, I drove to the seaside town of Santa Cruz, to the bead
store that Mark called the "jewel store," where he loved to pick
out rubies, sapphires, emeralds, pearls, and diamonds, all made
of glass or plastic. We'd often used them for games we invented,
like "jewel thief"; now I brought back a small brown paper bag full.
Joined by my brother and sister-in-law, and Rebekah, Heinz and
I walked together through the fields, by the paddock where the
horses came to the fence to greet us, to the fallen log that served
as our airplane, the apple tree, the tree house, and the creek. Each
of us took a handful of jewels and left them in the places that held
our memories, acknowledging what we'd shared there with Mark
every summer during the six years of his life.

We were exhausted with grief, and devastated, of course, but
grateful for what Rebekah's mother, a psychology professor at the
local university, told us. "Whenever I've known of the death of a
child, the parents either tried to ignore what happened, and it ru-

ined their lives—or else they turned it into the centerpiece, and it ruined their lives. But," she said, "you haven't done either; you'll be able to go on living, even though you're torn apart with grief." Having lived with Mark's impending death over us for years, we did feel some reassurance: nothing worse could happen.

We could not go back to our summer home in the mountains, having rented it out before Mark died; so when we flew back to Colorado we found a small apartment in town, where Heinz could easily ride his bicycle to the Center for Physics. We joined in picnics on Friday afternoons with the gathered tribe of physicists, and shared the Fourth of July parade and then the fireworks at parties with them, as well as with friends among the musicians who played at the music festival, and with those who lived in town. Heinz dived into conversations about physics, relieved to be back in the mountains, where he hiked with friends every Wednesday and Saturday. I spent days with Sarah, who by now, at thirteen months, was walking and running, eager—and fearless—to greet every dog we met. When we visited our friends in town, she would crawl under the bureau, intent on pursuing the cat who'd escaped there to hide. We spent hours by the creek, wading, and playing hide-and-seek outdoors in the meadows. After dinner, we'd walk to the park, Sarah riding on Heinz's shoulders, where there were swings, jungle gyms to climb, and a fountain where children ran, shrieking when the water suddenly shot up and splashed them. To anyone passing on the street, those summer days may have looked nearly normal.

When well-meaning friends tried to soften what happened, speaking of "the loss of your son," I inwardly froze, then flashed with anger. I didn't *lose* my child, like a mother distracted while shopping: he *died*! Yet beneath the anger ran an electric current of guilt. Wasn't protecting Mark's life our primary responsibility? Since we couldn't save his life, hadn't we failed as parents? What Heinz had said kept echoing in my mind: "I would have given my life for him—but no one would take it." Although he clearly meant it, he worked hard to bear his grief with the stoic reserve conventionally expected of men, which he also demanded of himself. I knew, of course, that he was grieving, brokenhearted, although not depressed; but I often felt overwhelmed. Every night after dinner I'd go outside the house to sit on the deck, wrapped in a blanket, listening to the rush of the creek and the wind in the forests, under a clear sky brilliant with stars, to meditate as the monks had taught me to do. Twenty-five years earlier, our friends Robert and Lucy Mann had introduced us to the Cistercian monks of St. Benedict's Monastery, often called Trappists, who live in the Colorado mountains in Snowmass, not far from Aspen. Bobby liked to joke that they'd invited him to become their first Jewish monk! But after he'd repeatedly invited the monks to come to his concerts at the Aspen Music Festival, he asked why they never came, and discovered that a monastic vow of stability bound them to stay at the monastery. So he offered to bring the music to them, playing in the monastery refectory, and we felt lucky to be invited with a few other friends to join them. At that first recital, Bobby played solo violin, while, at intervals, Lucy read Bible passages that they had chosen. After that, I often returned for evening mass to that place of deep peace among the mountains, and I came to know many of them as friends. Thomas Keating, formerly the abbot, asked me to come and meet with the brothers to speak about the *Gospel of Thomas*. But I said, "Instead of talking about it, I'll give each of you a copy," opening an intense discussion, since they immediately recognized it as a work of contemplative devotion—one that Christian monks in Egypt had read in their evening devotions thousands of years before. Sensing the depth of the Cistercians' devotional practice, I learned from Father Thomas what he taught of meditation and contemplative prayer, which helped calm emotional turbulence. The monks offered silent, unspoken support, never speaking to fill an awkward silence or saying things meant to sound hopeful, as many others did, like, "Your faith surely must have sustained you." What did they mean—a set of beliefs? Whatever most people mean by faith was never more remote than during times of mourning, when professions of faith in God sounded only like unintelligible noise, heard from the bottom of the sea.

That summer, when Emily and Lizzie came to visit us in the mountains, we took them to the Pine Creek Cookhouse for dinner, taking turns holding Sarah as we ate and talked. While I was at home with Sarah, Heinz took them to our favorite places, to the wildflower meadows below Cathedral Lake; to Woody Creek Tavern for enchiladas and beer; to Maroon Lake, mirroring mountain peaks still covered with snow. Later we hiked together, with Sarah in a child's backpack, through aspen forests and boulder fields to Crater Lake, and went to the music tent to hear Midori, a prodigy violinist, then eleven years old, play a Brahms violin concerto with passionate concentration and fervor.

Shortly after we flew back to New York, turning onto crowded highways to drive from the airport into the city, I prepared to start the new semester's teaching. Since I had accepted a position at Princeton, but didn't then have energy to teach, the department chairman asked me instead to lead discussion groups for a colleague's class. Waking to an alarm at five A.M., I would dress in the dark, quietly, to avoid waking Heinz and

Sarah, walk downstairs, and into the wet, gray New York streets toward Penn Station. There I'd join the crowds pressing toward the tracks, and step across the platform onto the New Jersey Transit train that swayed, lurched, and clattered suddenly from the black tunnel underneath the river into light, as the car hurtled through fields of reeds and marshes near New York, sometimes offering a glimpse of a white heron, then through backyards, empty factories with broken windows, lots dense with weeds and paper, cans, tricycles left in the rain, plastic wading pools, garbage cans, swing sets, some with ropes dangling loosely, the seats down. When I was lucky enough to find a seat, I'd turn my face to the window to hide the tears, struggling with questions that seemed to arise instinctively: Why did this happen? Why to this child? Why to *any* child, any person?

Body and mind felt discordant, separate islands of feeling, sharp with pain, interspersed with patches where feeling had numbed, wholly blocked. To screen out the screeching of the train wheels, I'd pull out my CD player and plug in earphones, to listen to the only music that I could tolerate during those years: Beethoven's late quartets. Since my arteries felt tangled and separate, in danger of disintegrating, I felt that only the strands of that music could help weave them together again, perhaps could bring, for moments, a semblance of integration and order. Focusing on our topics of discussion for the precept seemed impossible before arriving at Princeton Junction. But when I walked into the familiar seminar room, which smelled of old wood and chalk, and met the students, the class would set a boundary to those waves of choppy, deep waters. During those hours, the questions our students raised about the sources we were reading about interactions between Jews and Christians, their intense response to disagreements and bursts of laughter, felt like respite, recalling me to work that I loved.

Heinz always maintained more emotional balance than I did. Devoted to Mark, he now turned his devotion to Sarah and me, and I was moved to see him open up new depths of feeling for other people and for their children. When a member of his staff at the New York Academy of Sciences, which he now served as president, told him about his own child's difficult diagnosis, Heinz talked with him at length, helped him find the best medical care, and wept that he could not do more.

One cold winter afternoon, when we went to a Valentine's Day party at the loft that our close friends Lizzie and Emily shared, I heard him talking, loud, too loud, dominating a conversation. That hadn't happened for years; something was wrong. Later, upset and irritated by his behavior, I sensed that he was smoldering inside. After waiting for several hours, I finally told him how I'd seen him that afternoon, guessing that it was about Mark, that he was grieving unbearably, without acknowledging it. I'd expected that he might be angry; but at first he said nothing, and then, to my surprise, he said quietly, "Thank you for telling me that."

About a year later, as the turmoil slightly lessened, I turned back to what I'd been writing. Once again, raw experience poured into the work: grief laced with guilt cut especially deep. Before Mark's death, I'd begun to investigate how Jews and Christians deployed the story of Adam and Eve to sanction—and to censor—sexual practices. But now I was driven toward the primary questions that story addresses: Why do we suffer, and why do we die?

At the same time, a more intimate question pressed into the foreground: Why do we feel guilty, even when we've done nothing to bring on illness or death—even when we've done everything possible to prevent it? Suffering feels like punishment, as cultural anthropologists observe; no doubt that's one reason why people still tell the story of Adam and Eve, which interprets suffering that way. Claiming that "in the beginning" God created a perfect world, the story suggests that human choice—the choice to sin—brought death into the world, along with everything we suffer, from drought and famine to miscarriage, fever, insanity, paralysis, and cancer.

This, of course, is an ancient folktale that rationalists dismiss, like the African tale that claims to tell how death began: the snake whom the gods sent to bring immortality to humans got lost on the way and failed to deliver the gift. Since our everyday experience shows that we're a fragile, mortal species like any other, why do people still keep telling and retelling stories that blatantly contradict that experience? Or do stories like that emerge from our stubborn instinct of denial, as with Mark Twain, who joked that "I know that everyone dies, but I always thought an exception would be made in my case"?

But it's not only traditionally minded Christians who interpret suffering and death as punishment. Over two and a half thousand years ago, Israel's greatest prophets—Amos, Isaiah, Jeremiah—interpreted their peoples' disastrous defeats in war as divine punishment for failing to worship God and obey his commands. Biblical stories often suggest that those who die in an earthquake or flood, volcanic eruption, or through catastrophic illness—even children mauled to death by wild bears, for making fun of the prophet Elisha's baldness!—are suffering exactly what they deserve.

Or is guilt simply a reflexive response to loss that groups throughout the world interpret in ways that reinforce their cultural norms? I wondered that when I saw an inscription in a Greek temple built thousands of years ago to honor Asclepius, the god of healing. Set up by two brothers mourning their father, who had been attacked and killed by a wild animal, this inscription shows that they were convinced that the gods had sent his death to punish his—and their—secret sins. They ordered this inscription to publicly confess that they, and perhaps their father, had neglected the gods; and they placed it in the temple to show that now they were seeking to appease the gods by offering sacrifices, and to warn others to do the same. Even now, people in various cultures often seek to deal with illness by repenting of sins that they fear may have caused it. One Hopi story, for example, tells how a child bitten by a poisonous spider hovers between life and death while his father desperately consults a tribal healer. Told that he's brought this danger on his son by failing to prepare ritual ornaments for Spider Woman, the tribe's protector, the father immediately seeks to remedy his fault, so that his son might recover.

Was the guilt that weighed like a stone on my grief a legacy of Western culture, a hangover from ancient folktales? Do such stories articulate unconsciously held attitudes that may affect us long after we've rationally dismissed them? What startled me more than anything else was how my own emotions could pour into scenarios told in stories I didn't believe in. Yet guilt also seems to shadow people who have no use for religion: the very word we use for disease, "illness," derives from the Old English term "evilness." And even though blaming the victim—or the victim's parents—may be absurd, rationally speaking, how often, in emergency rooms, do we hear the question, whether unspoken or spoken out loud, "How could this happen? What has *he* done, *she* done, what have *we* done, to deserve *this*?"

Shaken by emotional storms, I realized that choosing to feel guilt, however painful, somehow seemed to offer reassurance that such events did not happen at random. During those dark, interminable days of Mark's illness, I couldn't help imagining that somehow I'd caused it. If guilt is the price we pay for the illusion that we have some control over nature, many of us are willing to pay it. I was. To begin to release the weight of guilt, I had to let go of whatever illusion of control it pretended to offer, and acknowledge that pain and death are as natural as birth, woven inseparably into our human nature.

Realizing this, Freud declared that humans created the gods out of fear—repeating what the Roman poet Lucretius said thousands of years earlier. When popularizing the teaching of his mentor, the philosopher Epicurus, Lucretius wrote, "Poor humankind, to have invented the gods, and thrown in a bad temper as well!" Like Lucretius, Freud suggested that if we believe that gods inflict earthquakes, floods, and lightning strikes, we may imagine that we can do something about what's beyond our control; at least we can seek to pacify the gods with offerings and prayer. Like Freud, Lucretius hoped to liberate people from religion, which he saw simply as a web of illusion, invented by children afraid of the dark.

But whatever the rationalists say, and whatever the doctors could tell us about how cells break down, nothing they said could satisfy the need to find meaning. After Mark's death, someone reaching for something "nice" to say assured me that surely his death would teach us some "spiritual lesson," so that we could "find meaning" denied to more fortunate parents like herself. I was furious, speechless with anger. *Schadenfreude*, I thought; she's congratulating herself on her own good luck at our expense, and she doesn't even realize it. Doesn't she know that suffering can shrivel hope, break hearts? Even if she hadn't just spouted a sentimental cliché, how *dare* she suggest that any benefit to us could possibly be worth a child's life? *Find* meaning?

What *is* clear is that meaning may not be something we *find*. We found no meaning in our son's death, or in the deaths of countless others. The most we could hope was that we might be able to *create* meaning. I was moved by what another bereaved mother, Maria of Paris, a Russian Christian whom Orthodox Christians revere as a saint, wrote after her six-year-old daughter died; she felt her "whole natural life . . . shaken . . . disintegrated; desires have gone . . . meaning has lost its meaning." But instead of sinking into passivity, she risked her life to save the lives of other people's children during the Nazi occupation. When German soldiers forced Jews into a central square of Paris before shoving them into trains hurtling toward the death camps, Maria slipped into the square to join them. There, whispering hastily, she persuaded several parents to allow her to hide their children in garbage bins, and so to save their lives, which she did, finding families to care for each one of them. Later, when she and her own son were arrested by Nazi soldiers and sent to the death camps, she exchanged places with someone targeted for the gas chambers, serene in the conviction that she'd done what her faith required, choosing to enable others to live. Many other parents whose children have been killed by gun violence, war, drunk drivers, or disease also choose to *create* meaning by working to spare other people unfathomable losses like their own.

Recently I read an article in the *New York Times* by a writer speaking of his young son's death, in which he characterized a decision he made with his wife to have another child as a "wild and daring act of courage." Certainly loving anyone as much as we love our children, then consciously choosing to risk another such loss, *does* take courage. But, I thought, doesn't he realize how fortunate he is to have such a possibility—one that so many bereaved parents don't have? Heinz and I felt intensely grateful that we were still young enough to hope for another child, or, better, more children, in our lives. Meanwhile, the work I'd chosen also felt like a kind of yoga, a practice of focus and discovery that can show how countless people throughout the ages contend with questions of meaning—perhaps even a way of spinning straw into gold, like Rumpelstiltskin.

But what mattered more than anything else was loving Mark. Then, after a miscarriage, we strongly felt that loving him so passionately *required* us to care for children, any child who needed parents—especially Sarah, whom we needed as much as she needed us. Now that she was one and a half years old, exploring her own young life, Heinz often carried her on his shoulders when we walked to the playground near us in Central Park. On weekdays, when he was at work at Rockefeller University or the New York Academy of Sciences, I'd take her in the stroller to the park, where I'd help her onto the swings and down the slides. On the walk home, she would stop at every staircase we passed, to climb up and down; then, laughing with surprise when pigeons scattered before her stroller, she greeted every squirrel and dog.

One year after Mark died, I felt that I could ask Heinz the question I'd waited to ask him for months: Shall we call the adoption agency to ask whether they'd include us again on their list of prospective parents? When we did, they said, "We thought you'd be calling," and one year later, to our delight, Sarah's younger brother, David, arrived to join our family in the spring.

CHAPTER 5

Unimaginable

Heinz Pagels in Castle Creek, Colorado, one week before his death on
July 23, 1988.

After the plane touched down in Aspen in light rain, sunlight glancing off the mountains, we gathered Sarah, hugging her indispensable bear, along with blankets, bottles, and David, and carried the children onto the tarmac. Heading first for the Center for Physics to pick up the information packet for summer events, we saw friends from Chicago in the parking lot. Heinz stopped the car and ran out to greet David Schramm, saying, "We have a little David now, too!"

This would be the first summer that we would live in the simple frame house we'd built in the mountains, at an altitude that could have put Mark at risk, over nine thousand feet, among the aspen and pine forests of Castle Creek valley. After packing the car with bags of groceries, we drove up to the house, listening to the rushing waters of the creek. The afternoon had turned gloriously clear.

When we went to picnics at the Center for Physics with other families, our friends, relieved to see us back, would come to admire our new baby, now six weeks old, as we set out fresh bread, salad, and chicken for our picnic and scrambled after Sarah, who would join other children, jumping over the tiny creek that ran through the grounds, then pull off her shoes to wade barefoot.

In June, before we'd left New York, Heinz's friends from the International League for Human Rights had given us a joint book party, made more joyous by the presence of a Soviet dissident newly freed from prison, who celebrated with us and spoke movingly of his gratitude. Each of us had just finished a book that we'd been working on for years. Heinz wrote about the potential for artificial intelligence in the book he called *The Dreams of Reason*—his kind of joke, since he'd borrowed the title from what sounds like an optimistic phrase from the Spanish painter Goya, who'd famously said that "the dreams of reason bring forth monsters." My book, *Adam, Eve, and the Serpent*, which began as an exploration of sexual attitudes and politics, had ended with a strong critique of Augustine's bizarre claim that "original sin" infected the whole human race and caused death—the final chapters "written with blood," Heinz said when he read them, and that's how they felt, shaped through Mark's illness and death. Both of us dedicated our books to Mark.

As we settled into our mountain home with Sarah and David, the pressures we'd lived with for so long began to ease. Every morning, Heinz rode his bike down the valley to the Center for Physics, and when he came home in the late afternoon, we'd drive up the road to the old mining town of Ashcroft to walk by the creek, where we often played hide-and-seek. Astonished to have lived through what we could not have imagined surviving, we occupied our days and nights with our children, with friends, and, when the children were asleep, talking close together by the fireside. On clear nights, when emotions poured through me, I'd go outside to sit on the deck as before, to allow grief to flow, and to meditate under the stars. The previous year, when Heinz went hiking on mountain trails—only for hiking had I ever seen him get up at five A.M.—I was worried about his safety, sensing how he was devastated with grief. This year, though, I breathed with relief, seeing his face sometimes light up again with flashes of humor and delight.

In early June, Heinz flew back to New York to speak at the graduation of Seth Lloyd, his doctoral student who'd just completed his PhD in physics at Rockefeller University. When he returned, I mentioned that I'd made a dinner reservation for us at our favorite restaurant in town. Startled, somewhat abashed, he asked, "Is this our anniversary?" I laughed. "That was last week, when you were in New York, but we can celebrate now."

A friend who'd seen us the week before, walking on the boarded path at Ashcroft, sent a photo she'd taken—Sarah riding on Heinz's shoulders, while I carried David—adding, in her note, "What a lovely family!" Glad to be back in our home again, we savored the clear summer days, often punctuated with rainstorms in late afternoon, before the sun would return in brilliantly clear air. One afternoon in mid-July, when Heinz came back from a bike ride with friends up the road for lunch, his knees were bruised and bleeding. He explained that he'd taken a fall on a hillside covered with gravel and rocks; it was, he insisted, nothing important.

Driving back home on Castle Creek Road to make dinner the next Friday, I was listening on the radio to news of a hang glider who'd fallen into a tangle of trees above the meadow where I was driving. Was he going to survive? So far, we didn't know; later we were glad to hear that he did. As I drove up to the house, listening to news reporting the difficulties of dating in a time of AIDS, I breathed a sigh of gratitude that I'd never have to think about anything like that. After what we'd been through this year, and as we are now, I knew we'd always be together.

Friends came to join us that night for dinner, the table piled with artichokes, grilled salmon, and fresh garlic bread for eight, besides the children. Heinz's former graduate student Seth was there, excited to be starting at the Center for Physics as one of the newest members of the tribe, and looking forward to hiking with Heinz in the morning. After dinner, when I was about to put Sarah to bed, Heinz offered to simplify our bedtime ritual by taking our friends out to walk up the road in the moonlight. So he said, "I'll take the kid," and carried David with him as they went to look at the stars. Then, Sarah and I piled into her bed next to her small mountain of stuffed animals while I told her stories and sang our song about the foxes, bears, bugs, and other creatures going to sleep—as long as it took, as I did every night, before she'd fall asleep.

When the alarm clock rang at five the next morning, I hugged Heinz as he got up to hike, then went back to sleep until David, sleeping in a crib in the bedroom's walk-in closet, woke me a couple of hours later. Hearing us stir, Sarah carried Bear upstairs to join us. On that sunny July morning, anticipating that Heinz would be hungry when he got back, I decided to make lasagna for dinner. Sarah sat near me on the kitchen counter to watch as I grated parmesan cheese and built up layers of pasta, meat sauce, and mozzarella.

Usually the hikers were back by early afternoon. Instead, the phone rang, and Sarah remembers feeling confused and upset at what followed. I called our neighbor Alice, asking her to come to stay with the children, and immediately left the house. He'd fallen—what could that mean? Seth made it back to Maroon Lake, told the rangers that the rocky path on which they were descending from Pyramid Peak suddenly gave way when Heinz, walking ahead of him, stepped on it, and fell down the mountain. No other information. About half an hour later, we heard overhead the ominous buzz of helicopters heading from town toward the Maroon Bells, signaling that members of the mountain rescue team were looking for a lost or fallen hiker. Were they looking for him? If he were badly hurt, I might have to spend the night at the hospital, so I called Alice to ask, "If that's what happened, would you look after the children?" She would.

Waiting. What if he'd broken his neck, or his spine? Would he be a paraplegic? That seemed impossible for such an active man—but, I thought, he'd still be Heinz: we'd find a way to live with it. Charged with adrenaline, I paced, went outside, then back in; there was nowhere to flee, no one to fight. That day had dawned into a brilliantly clear blue sky, but now the sky seemed to have gone blank. An hour passed, then two more; we could hear nothing but wind in the trees as we scanned the empty sky. I called emergency services, but the line was busy; when someone finally answered, he could tell us nothing. Did I call Lizzie and Emily in New York, to tell them that Heinz had fallen? I didn't remember. Apparently I'd called Katie and Tom Benton, who had been at dinner with us the night before, since they arrived at our door. How badly injured could he be? In case we'd have to stay at the hospital overnight, I packed a canvas bag and placed it by the door.

Late afternoon, nearly evening, and no phone call. Seth arrived, looking sober, distraught, behind him, someone with whom he was staying, and two policemen. I don't remember anything they said, until one of the policeman, perhaps summoning his best console-the-widow voice, said, "God never gives us more than we can handle." From shock, that triggered fury. *How dare you speak of this as a gift from God? What do you know of what I can—or cannot—handle? Have you any idea that our six-year-old son died a year ago?* But I said nothing. Unable to utter a word, I grasped with both hands the handle of the door near the deck where I was standing, and wrenched the door off its hinges. After that, I remember nearly nothing: a black hole had opened up and swallowed our life. Other people were bustling around the house; who were they? Sarah, confused, came looking for me, and I comforted her as well as I could, but I felt as if I weren't present. Mute as a stone, I could neither speak nor cry. *If I start to wail and weep*, I thought, *I'll never be able to stop*.

Just before dark, a call. They'd found Heinz's body and taken it to the hospital. Now they were preparing to transport it to the funeral home down valley, in Glenwood Springs. "No," I said, "you are not going to do that. You keep it right there. I'm coming to the hospital right now." Our friends drove; I could not have trusted myself on the road. Entering through the door of the emergency room, we were taken through blank corridors to a back room in the hospital, built with gray cement blocks, where a black canvas body bag lay on a table. "Ordinarily," the doctor said, "I'd strongly advise you to see his body, but in this case, you cannot. They found it in fragments." Unable to see it, I went to the body bag and felt it. Under the slick black canvas, I seemed to feel the flesh of a thigh, and perhaps a lower leg. After some time I finally left the back room, numb. They steered me into a room where I signed a paper giving permission for them to transport his body to Glenwood. But not for cremation, or not yet, although that's what Heinz had chosen for Mark, and what I'd agreed to allow after our son's funeral, since it seemed to offer Heinz some slight consolation. But this time, too, I resolved that we would have a funeral with his body present, not a "service of thanksgiving for the life"—nothing to disguise the horror of his death.

Much later, our friend Tom, who had driven me and his wife to the hospital, told me that when others were out of the room, he'd quickly unzipped part of the body bag. "They were right," he said, "You did not need to see that." Years later, he told me that when he'd first heard that Heinz had fallen, he knew that he must be dead, since no one could survive a fall from Pyramid Peak, but he hadn't dared tell me. When we arrived back at the house, realizing that Sarah needed care, her bedtime ritual, some semblance of normal, I seemed to come partly out of a state of shock. For despite the attention others lavished on her, she was wandering through the house, troubled and crying, sensing that everything had changed, all the grown-ups acting strange—her mother distracted, her father not home. Caring for David was simpler; after I fed and held him, walking and singing, he would sleep.

Meanwhile, my whole body remained on high alert. Although most of my brain seemed obliterated, the fraction that functioned felt wide awake, focusing on what needed to be done. What about Heinz's mother? Suddenly I realized that two policemen might arrive at her door in the peaceful suburbs of Philadelphia, like those who had arrived to tell me. That would be awful; somehow, she needed to have someone she trusted with her before hearing this from the police, or on the news. Should I call? Since I could not speak without bursting into tears and sobbing uncontrollably, I could not say what would tear her apart, as it had me. Like me, she would hear the news alone; how could she possibly bear it? She would need people with her, close friends. So I found the phone number of Heinz's friend and colleague Gino Segrè, who lived in Philadelphia, and called to tell him what had happened. Would he and his wife drive to Heinz's mother's home, after asking her closest friend to meet them there, so that they could support her when she would have to hear it? He would, and they did. Meanwhile, both of the children were crying, needing reassurance. I tried to give it, holding and soothing each of them so that they could sleep.

Finally, at three in the morning, alone in our bed, I kept turning to where he slept. Why wasn't he there? Couldn't we stop this from happening? Where had he gone? Sleep had fled: I lay awake, alert, shocked, expecting him to return; it must be a mistake. A tape loop had started in my mind, picturing him falling from Pyramid Peak, a scene repeating over and over, nearly every second, several times at every breath. About an hour later, Sarah found her way to my room in the dark, crying and clutching at me, touching my face, as if to see whether I was there, and whether I was alive; startled, I reacted with shock and anger.

Who told our friends? Had I called them? I wasn't sure, and I didn't think to ask. But soon friends unexpectedly arrived: our friend Lizzie, and our children's other godparents, Sharon and David, from New York; Richard, my high school boyfriend; and Linda, my college roommate and longtime friend from California. Nick Khoury, Heinz's closest colleague at Rockefeller, arrived with his wife after a day of hectic travel, having heard of the accident on the news while on a canoe trip in the Canadian wilderness. And to my surprise, three colleagues from Princeton, John Gager, Al Raboteau, and Jeff Stout, miraculously appeared the next day, like heroes. A science writer who loved Heinz had written an obituary in the *New York Times* that I saw much later, accompanied by a beautiful photo; other people later told me that they'd seen a notice in *Time* magazine.

For days I could not sleep, except perhaps in momentary snatches. So long as I stayed awake, I could imagine that what happened was only a nightmare from which, surely, I would wake up. When for moments I dropped off, I'd spend them with

Heinz, alive and fully present, then wake with sudden shock—was it still true, had it actually happened, that our world had shattered when his body shattered on the rocks? A funeral: What to do? Three endless days and nights after Heinz's death, unable to sleep, slightly fortified by the presence of close friends who drove me down to the Episcopal church, I went with them to arrange for a service. Nothing but music, I insisted, and the simplest prayer book service, like our marriage, except that we'd leave time for people who wanted to speak to do so. Friends in town offered to invite people to their nearby home afterward, to eat, drink, and talk—yes, thank you; we'd need that, too.

Right after meeting with the Episcopal priest to make the arrangements for the service, and for his body to be brought in a simple coffin—no euphemisms, it's about death—we drove out to the Trappist monastery at Snowmass, where our friend Brother Theophane, whose monastic name means "God manifest," silently stood waiting, tall, bent, and bearded. I walked into the chapel with Theophane, who lit the large single candle reserved for prayer for the dead, and we sat together in silence. His presence, sitting motionless in prayer, opened a deep well of quiet.

After more than an hour, for the first time in three days, I felt some of the vigilance drain out of my body. Enveloped by that silence, I slowly allowed myself to move into it. When that happened, I somehow felt as if I could speak to Heinz. Internally I cried out, "So how do *you* feel about this?" Of course, I expected no reply. If asked, I would have said that any hint of a response could only be projection. But quick as a shot, I heard a voice—internally, not out loud—saying, "This is fine with me; it's *you* I'm concerned about now." Too shocked and angry to register astonishment, I said—internally, again—"*Fine with you?* You leave me here with two babies, and it's *fine with you*?" When I realized what I was saying, I was completely taken by surprise. How could this be my own mind talking back to me, when I could never have come up with what I'd heard? What had happened was by no means *fine with me* then, nor is it to this day, nearly three decades later. What startled me most is that, unexpected as these words were, they *did* sound like something that he might say. I did not know what to make of it, and I left the monastery shaken with wonder.

On the day of the funeral, I went downstairs in the house, surprised to find a friend who'd just arrived from New York ironing a blouse for me to wear. Sarah and David would stay with our neighbor Alice, who would bring them to the gathering afterward. Walking into the small church, I noted that the coffin had been placed below the altar, the windows above opening onto trees and sky. We took our seats in the front row, as friends from the Center for Physics, from the town, and from all over packed the church. Lizzie later told me that she saw me holding on to the metal coffin throughout the service. I do not remember that, nor, as others later told me, that the Trappist monks had come, and sat together in a row near the front, dressed in their work clothes, jeans, flannel shirts, and boots instead of the white wool monastic robes that would have made their presence conspicuous, perhaps because they had taken a vow that ordinarily requires them to stay at the monastery.

The service went as planned, until the officiating priest began to preach—which I'd specifically asked him not to do—urging the congregation not to be angry with God. *Angry with God?* Doesn't he realize that many of these people are *physicists*, that most of them have never been in any church—that he's talking condescending nonsense? As he droned on, I became so angry with *him* that I crouched down and held myself fiercely in place, praying that he'd stop before I'd leap up and throttle him. Finally he caught my eye and quit. Then friends stood and spoke, words that I do not remember, but welcome words, spoken through love and grief. Last of all, Seth, who'd said that he wouldn't be able to speak but offered to make music instead, surprised us—and himself—by walking down from the loft where he'd been playing the flute. Standing in front, next to the coffin, he told us about the wonderful day they'd had, climbing to the top of Pyramid Peak, eating lunch in a meadow while looking out over the glorious mountains and valley, talking and joking before they started their descent. When Seth finished speaking, there was silence; we all sensed that the service was over. We embraced, cried, laughed, hugged, and talked, and swarmed over to the lavish garden where our friends had prepared a simple and lovely feast.

A few days later, Father Joseph, the abbot at St. Benedict's monastery, called to say that the monks would like to offer a mass for Heinz. Touched by their generosity, since they knew that Heinz was certainly not a Catholic, and likely would not have identified as Christian, I went to the monastery with a few friends one clear summer evening. While a friend carried David and held Sarah's hand as they walked outside among the fields and trees, we walked through the silent corridors into the simple brick chapel. After the usual prayers and readings, we sat in silence. Then, from that deep well of silence that often enveloped the monastery, Joseph spoke, perhaps for two minutes, in words as clear and simple as water. Having heard a child, whom he assumed was three-month-old David, crying in the hall outside the chapel, he said, "At this moment, we all feel like that child, crying in the hall; we don't understand; we are shaken with grief; we ask for the consolation of God's spirit." Afterward, I hugged and thanked him and the others, hugely grateful that their monastic practice allowed for such openhearted grace.

Later that week, I drove into town to go to an exercise class, having decided to do anything at all that might alleviate even the slightest fraction of the agony. But moments after starting to exercise, I suddenly felt faint and sat down. Then, to my horror, I saw that boils had raised all over my body. Hardly able to move, I called Katie, who arrived and immediately drove me to the hospital's emergency room. When a doctor came in, he surveyed the situation, gave me an injection, and asked what happened. Through storms of tears I stammered out what I could, adding defiantly, "I got through our son's death; I'll get through this." He stopped, and looked at me severely for a few moments. Then he said, "This is what we call acute traumatic stress reaction. Don't think that having survived your son's death makes you an expert. Actually, that makes it much worse."

During those strange, interminable evenings, when Heinz never came home, Seth came over nearly every night to keep us company, often playing on the floor with the children. After I put them to bed, we'd sit and talk. When Mark had died, Heinz and I shared together the grief we both felt. Now that he was gone, Seth and I sought some consolation talking for hours by the fireside, on nights when sleep had fled. We talked endlessly about what had happened during the hike, going over each detail again and again. We knew that Heinz had hiked that same trail many times before and was a careful climber. How, then, had this happened? Seth described how he first saw Heinz fall, how he uttered no sound, wholly focused instead on trying to grasp the ledge with his hands, but could not get a hold; how then he fell down about three hundred feet onto bare rock. He could not see what happened, but by then the men of mountain rescue had told us that his body went on falling for a thousand feet farther. Any sense of safety that I'd ever had shattered with him. I was overwhelmed to realize that the man whose enormous competence and care I'd counted on could have been, himself, so shockingly vulnerable. The images in my mind had never stopped since the accident; every few seconds I still could see him fall, over and over, a tape loop endlessly repeating.

One evening, our close friend Judith Schramm came over, having offered to help me sort out Heinz's papers, which I suddenly realized I could not have even touched by myself. We sat on the floor of the room he'd used as his office, with windows overlooking the forests and mountains, putting papers into cardboard boxes. The words of one letter he'd written two days before he died remained indelibly inscribed in my mind. Responding to an invitation to speak at a physics conference in Holland, he'd written a note to the colleague who'd invited him, saying,

> Dear Professor ——, Thank you for your kind invitation to speak at the physics conference in Amsterdam this fall. Although the topic sounds very interesting, I regret that I am unable to attend at this time. Since my wife and I have two small children, we never spend more than one day apart.

Heinz hadn't mentioned the invitation to me, and we'd never talked about an agreement like that, which was simply implicit in the choices we made and the way that we'd lived. Although to

this day I treasure what he wrote, I wanted to cry out and protest, "But now you've been gone for more than a whole week!"

Throughout those nameless days, my temper exploded at
slight frustrations. Trembling, starting in my stomach, would
spread until my whole body was shaking. On the floor, I'd bend
over involuntarily, head to the ground, emitting a strange keening sound I'd never heard before. Sometimes outbursts of sobs
began uncontrollably; more often, I'd try to cry, but no tears
would come. Although grieving and raging, I hardly dared feel
storms of rage, could not bear to turn against the man I'd loved
so dearly. *He's* the one who died, I thought; he hadn't intended to
die, surely didn't want to. I kept recalling what Seth told me, how
he'd spent the last seconds of his life desperately scrambling to
get a handhold. How, then, could we blame him? Nevertheless,
huge waves of emotion crashed over us. How could he have abandoned us now—just as we were starting to recover from Mark's
death? Why hadn't he thought of us when taking such risks with
his life? In snatches of sleep, I'd see him, overjoyed to see him
alive; but sometimes, in dreams, he'd turn away, inexplicably
indifferent, as he never did in life, leaving only desolation. Years
passed before I realized, through the help of someone who'd been
similarly bereaved, that sobs without tears are a form of anger.
Alone at night, I ferociously fought back tears, unable to cry; yet
even when breath, so often stopped and suppressed, turned into
bronchitis, then pneumonia, I resisted the tears, still feeling that
once they started, they'd never stop.

Finally, raw and desperate, I called a friend, saying, "You
know everyone in town; what therapist would you suggest I
see?" After she mentioned several names, she said of one, "Her
husband died in a plane crash when she had three small chil-

dren." "I'll go to her." When I did, the therapist, knowing what had happened, opened by saying, "You have no choice about how you feel about this. Your only choice is whether to feel it now or later." Although her comment helped a little at first, during the next twenty-five years I would keep discovering that how much I was able to feel, or not, and when, was not a matter of choice.

When Geoff West, Heinz's close friend since the time they studied physics together in graduate school, heard of his death, he'd called from Santa Fe, terribly shaken, saying that he would drive up to Colorado for the funeral. But since the house was packed, and knowing how many people would be there at that time, I asked him instead to come later, when others had left, so that we'd have time to spend together and to talk. When he did drive to Aspen, a couple of weeks after Heinz's death, he told me that when he'd first heard of it, he'd searched for a prayer shawl that he'd kept at the bottom of a drawer ever since his bar mitzvah. For although raised in an intensely orthodox family, decades earlier he'd left his family behind, along with their pieties, in London. On that day, however, he took the prayer shawl and kippot, drove alone out of town to climb to the top of a mesa, and began to chant the ancient tones of Kaddish, the prayer for the dead. He told me that when he began, the sky had been perfectly clear, but as he chanted, his voice hoarse and breaking, a dark gray rain cloud formed overhead; then sudden winds, drenched with rain, swept over the mesa. When he finished, the rain stopped, and the sky cleared. As he descended the mesa, he gathered a few small branches from a sage bush, which he brought to me.

Without such friends, I cannot imagine surviving that summer. For, I realized, if anything could destroy me, especially after Mark's death, it would be this. The long and loving relationship with Heinz had kept me balanced, as a parent, as a person. Going on without him felt impossible. He was so much the better parent, I felt; why weren't the children left with him instead? More than once, driving alone up the mountain road back to the house, I suddenly felt startled out of reverie, shocked: I was driving far too fast, and heedlessly; one absent moment could send the car careening over the cliff. It's not that I wanted to die, but desperately wanted to stop the pain, and that could drive an impulse toward suicide.

Although I dreaded going on, suicide was not an option. *It's no honor to Heinz to fall apart now*, I kept repeating to myself. He would not have quit, certainly not with children depending on us. Now I would have to go on, to "stand on the side of life," as he often said of people he respected. During those sleepless nights in August, around three or four in the morning, Gerard Manley Hopkins's words often echoed through my head:

> No, I'll not, carrion comfort, Despair, not feed on thee;
> Not untwist—slack they may be—these last strands of
>   man
> In me or, most weary, cry *I can no more*. I can;
> Can something, *hope,* wish day come,
> not choose not to be.

When longing for sleep, or for oblivion, I realized that if I hadn't stopped drinking alcohol before Mark died, I'd probably be trying to drink myself to sleep.

But there was a lot to do. Groceries, baths for the children, packing boxes to return to New York, others to leave in the storage room. What to do with his rugby shirt, his worn sneakers? Carefully I packed the belt he always wore, with the inlaid Zuni buckle that I'd given him years before on his birthday, and his watch, the leather strap stained with his sweat, which the mountain rescue team had recovered from the hike. I kept in the closet two of his shirts and his favorite sweater, which, when I buried my face in them, still breathed with his scent, and the black satin jacket with his name sewn onto it, a twin to mine, each with REALITY CLUB inscribed on the back.

Stopping at the local airport to check on tickets for return to New York—his ticket now blank, to be unused—I saw a young woman trying to quiet the baby strapped to her breast while a two-year-old, loudly protesting, grabbed her hand and pulled on it hard. That's just like me, I thought, that's what it looks like to have an infant and a two-year-old, about to board the plane. But right then her husband rushed to her side, holding tickets and baggage, and the similarity stopped. For us, there would be no husband. No longer married, suddenly I was *widowed*. From Latin, the name means "emptied." Far worse; it felt like being torn in half, ripped apart from the single functioning organism that had been our family, our lives. Shattered, the word kept recurring; the whole pattern shattered, just as the mountain rocks had shattered his body.

Much of what happened after that remains a blur. I do not remember traveling back to New York. The president of Princeton called to ask, "What can we do to help?" "Thank you," I said, thinking, *Nothing. There's nothing you can do to help, You can't bring him back.* Later, though, I called him to say that perhaps a stipend from the university's emergency fund could help me afford to see a psychiatrist. I knew that I could not possibly teach; the energy and clarity that teaching requires, which I'd always taken for granted, were gone. The department chairman arranged for others to give lectures, assigning me only the task of leading small discussion groups in classes taught by our colleagues. That much I could manage. Without that fragment of normal life to cling to, as well as the income it provided, I felt that I might go insane.

At first I was relieved to be back in New York, in our brownstone walk-up apartment with high ceilings, the flowered Persian carpet he'd bought at auction, which we called "our garden," and in our own bedroom—him so strangely absent—that looked out onto trees below. But what to do with the heavy mahogany box containing his ashes that arrived from Farnum Funeral Home in Glenwood Springs, along with three copies of a death certificate? Finally I placed it on top of the highest bookshelf, where no one would notice and no one else would know what it was. I wanted to keep anything of him that remained, however meager, near us.

Although I hoped to cling to some continuity, new concerns suddenly intruded. The lawyer who'd skillfully navigated our purchase and renovation of the rent-controlled apartment we'd moved into when we married more than twenty years earlier now told me that we could no longer afford to live there. The mortgage, our finances, the expenses, depended on both our salaries, now dropped to less than half when his salary ended; only mine remained. Even apart from expenses, I'd begun to realize that we could no longer go on living in New York. I could not leave our children in New York, even for a day, without a parent close by, although our beloved Jean was still caring for them in our home. Before, on the two or three days a week I went to

Princeton, Heinz had stayed home until around noon, return-ing home early from his office, since I could arrive in time for family dinner. Now I dreaded the thought of having to sell our apartment, leave everything familiar, our neighborhood and our friends, and find a place to live in a town we didn't know—another change that would further fracture the life we'd once shared.

Next, our lawyer called me into her office for more bad news, her desk and part of the floor covered with old tax returns and piles of financial records she'd found in Heinz's office. Twenty-four years earlier, before we married, when Heinz first moved to New York to take the position at Rockefeller University, he'd identified his mother, then his next of kin, as the sole beneficiary of his accumulated pension account and his life insurance pol-icy. So even though we'd been married for over twenty years, and had written our joint will as soon as Mark was born, he'd never thought to change it to include us as his beneficiaries.

That fall, Heinz's colleagues at the New York Academy called me to say that Andrei Sakharov, the Russian physicist once hon-ored in the Soviet Union for pioneering that country's nuclear research, whom the Soviet secret police later forcibly consigned to a mental hospital because he was publicly advocating for human rights, had been released, partly in response to sup-port that Heinz and other scientists had initiated through the International League for Human Rights. Now Sakharov and his wife, Yelena Bonner, were about to arrive in New York, and were planning to come to the New York Academy of Sciences, having intended to thank Heinz in person.

Nearly fifteen years earlier, the Soviet Academy of Science had invited Heinz to come for a scientific exchange with physicists in Russia. Out of courtesy to our hosts, we flew on Aeroflot, the Russian airline. When we arrived in Moscow, the airport police, poker faced and suspicious, harshly interrogated me about the sheaf of Coptic texts they discovered in my suitcase. What kind of code *was* this, anyway? Since Coptic, an ancient Egyptian language, looks rather like Greek and Russian, but deviates from both, they apparently assumed that I was working for the CIA. I told them that if they could read it better than I could, I'd love to have their translation. They were not amused, and harassed us for nearly four hours; but when they gave up, a Russian physicist drove us to our apartment in a cement building in the small city two hours from Moscow, where French physicists, collaborating with Russians, had built an atom smasher. "Don't worry; they won't bug our apartment," Heinz had assured me. "Everyone likes to say they've been bugged, to make themselves sound important, but we're not important enough for them to bother with." But when agents of the secret police confronted us in Moscow and demanded that we hand over books we'd brought to give to a famous Jewish physicist who had asked us for them, we realized that they'd overheard us talking in the apartment that the government assigned to us. Then Heinz said, "I get it—it's not about being important, it's about employment. The government has to employ everyone, so they *do* bug everyone!"

As Americans on a scientific exchange, often we were treated as highly privileged guests, immune from official threats, but soon we discovered what no one there would tell us. In the town where we lived, we saw a crew of Mongolians and other Asian men splitting railroad ties and building new tracks, as overseers with whips and guns stood over them and watched. When I asked the secret service agent assigned to me who those people were, she casually explained that they were part of an army—a "slave army," she said—conscripted and forced into hard labor. Although the scientists we knew were far more protected, since government officials regarded them as essential for military research, we quickly learned that Jewish scientists, often even the most prominent among them, constantly suffered from virulent—and institutionalized—anti-Semitism.

When Heinz was invited to speak at two different physics institutes in Moscow, we stumbled onto another secret. No one had ever told us that these institutes were segregated—one only for non-Jews, the other for Jews. Since Heinz wasn't Jewish, he was invited to both. When we went to the second, we were looking forward to seeing a famous physicist whom he knew. But when that physicist arrived to hear Heinz's talk, he came in late and left early, shaking his head and hurrying out to signal that we weren't to speak with him, since talking with us would be dangerous for him. Saddened to see him humiliated, we wondered what kind of threat could terrify a man who was one of Russia's most respected scientists. When Heinz confidentially inquired, a Russian colleague explained that Jewish physicists who displeased the secret police risked losing their apartments and having their children banned from attending any university. Others told us that some of the Jewish scientists had not been able to attend his talk, since they'd been denied visas to travel to Israel, or anywhere outside Russia, and had protested by starting a hunger strike. Shaken and troubled, Heinz resolved to do whatever he could to advocate for human rights, especially for his colleagues. "There's not much we can do," he said, "but we have to do whatever we can."

So after we returned to New York, he became actively involved in the International League for Human Rights, and later became its president. After gathering support from physicists in the American Academy of Sciences to publicize and protest the harsh discrimination that Jewish scientists experienced in the Soviet Union, he'd also initiated protests against the internment of Andrei Sakharov, intended to silence his influential voice. Now that Sakharov and his wife were soon to arrive in New York, having planned to meet Heinz, his colleagues at the academy asked me to meet with them instead. I took two-year-old Sarah with me, who was delighted to walk up and down the magnificent staircase with Heinz's secretary during the ceremony. When it was done, I walked into the hall and unexpectedly stood face-to-face with Heinz's portrait. Immediately I turned, blinded by tears, picked up Sarah, and left—the only time I ever went back there after he died.

The next challenge felt even worse, terrifying. Heinz's colleagues at Rockefeller had arranged a memorial service at the university, to be held toward the end of September—now coming up the next week. Since his death I had never gone back there either. The prospect of walking into his office, where I'd gone countless times to meet him, knowing that he would not be there, felt overwhelming—more inescapable evidence that he was not coming back. So I never went there; colleagues and friends packed his belongings and sent them to me. But I *would* have to go to the memorial service, and greet many people who had known and loved him, their simple presence reconfirming his death. Of course I could not deny what had happened, but I could hardly imagine walking into a public space filled with people who had come to acknowledge it.

The night before the service, deeply distraught, I answered the phone. Thomas Keating, Trappist monk and spiritual father of the Colorado monastery, called to say that he was in New York visiting his sister. "Might I stop by for a visit?" Surprised and relieved to hear his voice, I said, "Yes, of course, Thomas; I didn't know that monks made house calls!" When he arrived that evening after the children were asleep, he suggested that we meditate. When we did, his presence, like Theophane's in the monastery chapel, felt like a deep anchor into the unknown. After we sat together in silence for more than an hour, I asked about something strange that happened during the meditation. "Thomas, I felt as though waves of energy were coming toward me from various directions, like waves and ripples in an ocean, as though people were sending me energy; but I have no idea from whom they came. What—if anything—do you make of this?" Before that time, when someone said to me "I'm praying for you," I'd assumed that this was a vague gesture, a nod to good intentions, the pious equivalent of saying "Let's have lunch sometime." So that evening I was surprised, not having imagined that actual transactions might occur, as, in that extraordinarily susceptible state, I felt that they had. Thomas simply nodded and said, "Yes, that is what sometimes happens." Having spent over fifty years in contemplative practice, he seemed to inhabit such states of being, and find them familiar.

The next day, Heinz's mother arrived, somber and sad; she, too, held grief close with a stoic reserve. She had not been able to travel to Aspen for the funeral, after the sudden shock of his death, so we agreed to go together to the memorial service. As a young woman, daughter of a long line of Lutheran pastors, she'd left religion behind and turned instead to Goethe and Wagner, often quoting a saying she attributed to Nietzsche: "Whatever does not kill me, makes me stronger."

My own parents, living in California, had not come for the funeral, as they hadn't come for Mark's, and were not coming for the memorial service either. In moments of anguish I'd longed for them to come, despite having learned over and over, as a child, that looking to my mother for comfort was usually futile. She had not come to visit when Mark was born, or when he had open-heart surgery, or when he died, each time having murmured some forgettable excuse. This time, during those moments when I sank into devastation, I tried to buoy myself up by saying, "Just as well—if they were here, I'd have to take care of *them*." Only decades later, when our daughter, in her midtwenties, had twin babies born prematurely, did I realize how strange that was—and how shockingly painful. I could not imagine staying away from my own daughter at such a crucial time; how could any mother do that? But the pattern of oblivion was so deeply entrenched in our family that I allowed myself to be oblivious of that, too, until raw emotion burst out decades later.

So I was doubly grateful that Heinz's mother was coming. Ever since Heinz and I had become engaged, she'd welcomed me into her family, and I'd felt closer to her than to my own mother. Devastated as we both were now, we needed each other more than ever. I felt somewhat consoled to think that when we moved to Princeton, as we'd have to do now, we'd see her much more often; Sarah, too, was deeply attached to her "omma." But when we did, she could hardly bear to see us, and seldom did. To a considerable extent, she, too, sought to cope with Heinz's death by blocking it out; and apparently our presence recalled too intensely the son—and grandson—she'd lost.

From her reserve, holding herself away from close embraces, and from comments other family members made later, I finally realized that, perhaps obscurely, she partly blamed me. How had I allowed her son to engage in such dangerous sport? Why hadn't I stopped him? I'd asked myself the same questions and blamed myself as well. No matter that long before the time we met, Heinz loved to hike in the mountains, or that none of all our friends with whom he hiked for over twenty-two years had ever been seriously injured, much less killed. Despite the guilt that I now recognized as the underbelly of grief, I knew that no one who loved him could have changed that. Although his mother adored Heinz, her closest friend told me later that after he died she never mentioned his name again. Not long afterward, she herself became ill and died. And although her other son discouraged us from coming to see her, I went on my own when she was alone, in a coma, and sat with her for hours, holding her hand, sometimes speaking gently, with no perceptible response.

But on that clear September morning, I walked with her, holding her arm, through the iron gates of the university where we'd all danced together to celebrate our wedding. Entering the auditorium for the memorial service, which felt enormous, cavernous, on that day, I held my breath, fervently hoping to be able to greet people without starting to weep uncontrollably. Much of the service I don't remember, except that Heinz would have been surprised and moved to see that, along with so many other friends and colleagues, his thesis adviser from Stanford had flown across the country to speak so warmly of him for a few minutes. What especially opened my heart was hearing Robert Mann and the musicians he'd generously brought with him playing an exquisite movement of a Schubert string quartet, with passion that allowed our feelings to pour into the music.

A month or two later, our close friends Lizzie, Emily, Sharon, and David asked me to join them for dinner. As the children's godparents, they said, they'd been discussing our situation. Since the adoption agency finalized adoptions only after a child was a year old, they knew that we'd completed the legal process with Sarah but hadn't had time before Heinz died to complete it with David. They had met before our dinner and agreed to a difficult task: to tell me that I was in no condition to do so. Raising one child was hard enough, they said, but doing so alone, as a widow, now solely responsible for supporting this child emotionally and financially, was clearly overwhelming. Certainly I must not take on sole responsibility for two.

Shocked into silence, I finally spoke. "What are you saying? Do you have any idea how it feels to have lost Mark, then Heinz? You imagine I would—*voluntarily*—lose *another* of our children? That's insane!" They were trying to help, of course, but what they advised was impossible. Yet hearing their concern, I worried about how the social workers from the agency, soon to arrive in New York to evaluate the adoption, would see our situation. A few weeks later they came to New York and stayed for several days, spending many hours with each of the children, then sitting in our home observing Sarah and David with me and Jean, while interviewing us at length. To our enormous relief, they agreed to proceed.

Christmas lights, again, piercing like knives. The spirit of that season was never more remote than during those dark December days. Fortunately, Sarah, at two, and David, eight months old, did not notice the lapses. The date that loomed for me was New Year's Eve. From the start of our marriage, Heinz and I had always given a party with lots of dancing; after we had children, we'd meet with those two other couples, close friends, for a celebratory dinner, the six of us—now five. This time we met at a crowded New York restaurant. After nearly two hours pressed into a booth, forks and glasses clattering, and noisy, shouting talk all around us, I was relieved to have gotten through it and go home.

Waking alone in the dark early the next morning, New Year's Day, the coming year stretched out like a bleak and endless highway, leading nowhere. I kept walking back and forth, holding David to ease his pain from colic, while Sarah cried and screamed, clamoring for attention. Having held on for months, thinking that that *if only we can get through to the new year*, now I felt plunged into black ice, in danger of drowning. As the day wore on, in the solitude of our apartment, I felt flashes of horror: Is it possible that I couldn't—shouldn't—be trusted with our own children? Suddenly I understood our friends' concern. Could this be what precedes some kind of breakdown—a sudden shift to feel oblivion as temptation, even as seduction? Shaking, I called a friend and told her that I'd come close to a breaking point. "It's no honor to Heinz to fall apart now," I kept repeating. If he'd been left instead of me, he would have grieved and wept, then stopped crying, taken care of the children, and gone on, would have married again. I must honor our marriage, and our commitments to our children.

When my friend called back, she said, "Stay right there; I've arranged for someone to get there soon to help you."

"Where will she stay?"

"With you, of course."

The next day, Sarah Duben-Vaughn arrived on our doorstep, suitcase in hand, having just flown in from California. Plain, practical, and energetic, she sized us up and moved in. Sarah, startled to discover that there could be another Sarah, immediately named her "Other Sarah," responding to her generous warmth, as we all did. As tension began to drain from my body, I began to make sandwiches, with lemonade and chamomile tea, and to pack a bag for an afternoon at the park. That night, after the children had splashed and played in the bathtub, heard stories and songs, and finally slept, we talked until morning. A practicing psychologist, Sarah came from a family of nine, and had raised four children. Now, having gone through a divorce from a difficult marriage, she was willing to stay with us, to help. Before she arrived, I'd felt almost immobilized. Now we went out together, to the grocery store, to the cleaners, to the pediatrician's office. "People are going to think you're my nanny," I joked, "but I feel that you've saved my life!"

After about ten days, fortified by her presence, I began to clear the closets of some of Heinz's clothes. Carefully keeping the sweater he often wore, his rugby shirt, and the wedding clothes that smelled like him, I packed others to give to the Church of the Heavenly Rest, so that people who needed them could wear them. What about the heavy mahogany box on top of the bookcase? I could not imagine what to do, where it should go; yet after six months I felt its presence in our apartment weighing us down. When I finally confided in "Other Sarah" during one of our long evening talks, I realized that Heinz's physical remains belonged where together we'd placed those of Mark, in the columbarium—the "dovecote"—in the lower level of the church.

How to make this transition? When I called the priest at the church, he agreed to meet us on a Friday morning in January to receive the box, and to arrange for an interment ceremony. That day, after Jean came to take the children out for the morning,

"Other Sarah" offered to ritually cleanse and bless the house. Having brought sage from California, she burned it to create incense, then chanted prayers and blessings in every part of the home we had shared. We placed the heavy mahogany box in the center of the living room, and she incensed it as an orthodox priest would incense a coffin. Then we slowly carried it downstairs and out into falling snow, and turned toward Central Park. I'd refused to take a taxi, feeling that this mission required us to walk, and to carry the box ourselves.

Steadily falling at first, the snow softened all sound; we could hear the wind in the trees and see only our own footsteps in fresh snow. As we walked, increasingly braced against the wind, the storm intensified into a magnificent blizzard, which nearly emptied the park, turning it back into wilderness. Suddenly I recalled the day, over twenty years earlier, when Heinz had asked me to marry him—how then we'd walked out of his East Side apartment into snow falling in Central Park, toward the Museum of Natural History, arms around each other, filled with emotion, anticipating that we would marry. Now, on another Friday, also during the first week of January, Sarah and I were walking back the opposite way. Among waves of grief, I felt a surge of gratitude, thinking, *We kept our vows; we kept faith with each other.* After depositing the box with the priest to wait for the interment ceremony, we stopped to buy red tulips on the way back to the apartment. Now that was done.

CHAPTER 6

Life after Death

David Pagels's second birthday, with Elaine, Sarah, and Emily Raboteau and her family, in Princeton, New Jersey.

D o you believe in life after death?"

"Yes, of course—but not my life after my death."

Recalling Heinz's answer when someone had asked him that question, I thought, *So* that's *what we're living now—life after death.*

But how to go on? Questions kept recurring: Where do they go? How can someone so intensely alive suddenly be gone? What happens? Where are they? Somewhere, or nowhere? Flashes of insight would vanish, like water falling through my fingers, leaving only hints, guesses—and hopes. On the day Mark died, I'd been astonished to have the clear impression that after he initially departed from his failing body, he'd been invisibly present with us in a room down the hall, then had returned to his body when his heart started beating again, only to stop when his heart and lungs failed to circulate oxygen. Moments later, back in the room where his lifeless body lay, I felt that somehow I'd seen precisely where he had ascended to the ceiling in a swirl of silver energy and departed. And what had happened three days after Heinz died, when he'd seemed to answer my unspoken question? Both experiences were completely contrary to what I expected, yet both felt vividly real—neither, as I'd been taught to believe, simply illusions, or instinctive denial of death's finality.

More than six months after Heinz died, another surprise. I opened the top drawer of my bureau, looking for the comic picture of Superman emblazoned on a cover of *Time* magazine, titled "Superman at Fifty!," which I'd hidden there a year earlier to use on the invitations for the party I'd secretly planned for his fiftieth birthday. He never made it to fifty, though; that would have happened this February. Next to that picture, I'd placed the watch and belt that mountain rescue volunteers recovered from his body in July. Turning over his watch, I was astonished—not that it had stopped, but that it hadn't stopped soon after he died. Instead, the watch's timer showed that it had stopped one day before I was looking at it, on February 19—on the day that would have been his fiftieth birthday.

Could this be coincidence? Of course it could; I cannot draw any clear inferences from such incidents, although they'd shaken what once I'd taken for granted: the rationalism of those who insist that death is nothing but disintegration. As one anthropologist observes, when we confront the unknown, any interpretation is provisional, necessarily incomplete. Still, those experiences left with me the sense that when I come near death, I'll likely be hoping to see the two of them, as the song says, welcoming me to join them "across the shining river." At other times, though, I expect nothing more than a blank sky.

Meanwhile, there was work to do: raising our children, wading through a mass of legal papers, finances, and taxes, and recovering the professional life that was now our sole support, while, at a subterranean level, feeling adrift in dark, unknown waters. And although I'd flared with anger when the priest at Heinz's funeral had warned not to be "angry at God" because of his sudden and violent death, I struggled not to sink under currents of fear, anger, and confusion that roiled an ocean of grief.

At times I turned that anger on myself, especially when certain relatives would demand, "Why didn't you stop him from climbing?" implying that if I'd only done something different, he'd still be alive. At other times my anger turned toward him, when people raised accusing questions I'd suppressed: *Why weren't you more careful? Why didn't you realize what your death could do to our family?* After he died, one of his longtime hiking companions would cross the street whenever he saw me, to avoid speaking, apparently choosing to believe that the fall was Heinz's fault, as if no careful climber, like himself, ever risked such an accident. Or perhaps he simply refused to acknowledge the vulnerability that underlies everyday life, as I longed to do myself. Every time that vision of his fall recurred, it opened an abyss, revealing how fragile our lives are. When Seth and I talked late at night, he told me what he'd seen in those last moments: How Heinz had stepped onto a path he knew well, having hiked it many times. This time, apparently, ice had frozen into fissures in the rock, so that it suddenly fractured and gave way under his weight—from one point of view, a matter of simple physics. Yes, Heinz, I thought, you were working on chaos theory, and your death persuaded me of it, and of the randomness of events in the universe, of which you often spoke.

Weeks later, Jeremy Bernstein, the physicist with whom Heinz shared an office, as well as countless hikes and jokes, came to talk about something we'd both noticed: how his ankles bowed out as he walked. When Jeremy reminded me that Heinz had taken a surprising fall only weeks before his death, we began to piece that together with what Jeremy hadn't known: that he might have been losing strength from postpolio syndrome. For when Heinz was five years old, he lost sensation in his ankles and legs, and was diagnosed with polio; the doctors told his parents that he'd never walk again. He'd told me about the constant pain he'd endured as he lay in a hospital bed for over a year, dreading the agonizing spinal taps, immobilized on a ward with children trapped in iron lungs, terrified that he'd never get out. Every day his mother came to care for her son, encouraging him as he struggled to stand while grasping the iron bars of the hospital bed, teeth clenched with pain, until finally, with crutches and braces, he began to take steps.

By the time Heinz was in college, he'd become a strong, quick athlete who delighted in movement, and loved to hike, ski, and aim tennis balls across the court. In his forties, he brushed off what we'd heard of postpolio syndrome, which often occurs decades later to those who'd recovered from polio as children. If that's what happened, it could account for the bowed-out ankles and loss of balance. Yet even if so, knowing him, I realized that he would have ignored any twinges of pain, any slight imbalances, having overcome his vulnerability as a child through fierce determination to walk again.

We don't know for sure, of course, and even if we did, we'd still be left with emotional turmoil, like Sarah, who was racked with confusion, grief, and guilt, sometimes crying, sometimes furiously beating with her fists. No matter how much I held and rocked her, saying that he loved her, sometimes she'd blame herself, crying out, "Make Daddy come home—I'll be good!" More often, she'd go into closets to hide, ducking out for a moment to shout, "Daddy, come find me!" At times like that, I was amazed and moved, guessing that instead of being afraid that he'd left because she was bad, she'd apparently decided that he was playing our game of hide-and-seek, and needed more clues, since she was hiding so well that he couldn't find her. One afternoon in Colorado I drove out with her to the fields of tall grasses and wildflowers at Ashcroft, near Castle Creek, taking a picnic, as we'd often done as a family. When she initiated our game, hiding behind a tree and shouting, "Daddy, come find me!" I did the same. After we were both tired from running and shouting, hearing only the wind in the trees and the rushing creek, I gathered her into my arms, stroking her hair, and said, "Sarah, he would come to you if he could; but he can't come now."

But as Father Joseph had said during the mass at the St. Benedict's Monastery, we adults often feel just as children do. For although being "angry at God"—or at myself, or him, or anyone else—made no sense to me, I was often overwhelmed by sudden, intense bursts of anger that had no outlet, no appropriate target. The anguish brought by Mark's death, still fresh, now cut far deeper than ever. As long as Heinz was alive, we'd weathered and tempered each other's wild storms of emotion as we saw our child moving closer to death, experiencing grief primarily as sadness—unspeakable, unimaginable sorrow.

But this second loss, striking like lightning, ignited shock and anger beyond anything I'd ever imagined, and I fiercely resisted both. It wasn't just that my parents routinely stifled such feelings; much of our culture worked to shut them down. For as the anthropologist Renato Rosaldo notes in his powerful essay "Grief and a Headhunter's Rage":

> Although grief therapists routinely encourage awareness
> of anger among the bereaved, upper-middle-class Anglo-
> American culture tends to ignore the rage devastating
> losses can bring. . . . This culture's conventional wisdom
> usually denies the anger in grief.

In his essay Rosaldo tells how he'd shared such denial until a devastating loss shattered it. Before that, he says, when talking with men of the Ilongot tribe in the northern Philippines, he was at a loss to understand what motivated their tribal practice of headhunting. When asked, the men simply told him that grief—especially the sudden rupture of intimate relationships—impelled them to kill. Their culture encouraged the bereaved man to prepare by engaging in ritual, first swearing a sacred oath, then chanting to the spirit of his future victim. After that, he was sworn to ambush and kill the first person he met, cut off the head, and throw it away. Only this, his informants explained, could "carry his anger."

Dismissing what they told him, Rosaldo kept looking for more complicated, intellectually satisfying reasons to account for this ritual—until his young wife, the mother of their two children, accidently fell to her death. Finding her body, he says, the shock enraged and overwhelmed him with "powerful visceral emotional states . . . the deep cutting pain of sorrow almost beyond endurance, the cadaverous cold of realizing the finality of death . . . the mournful keening that started without my willing, and frequent tearful sobbing." At the time he wrote in his journal that, despairing and raging, he sometimes wished "for the Ilongot solution; they are much more in touch with reality than Christians. So I need a place to carry my anger—can we say that a solution of the imagination is better than theirs?"

His question challenged me: Are the elusive experiences noted above, which I dared hope hinted at something beyond death, nothing but denial—what Rosaldo derisively calls "a solution of the imagination"? Noting that some Ilongot men converted to Christianity after headhunting was outlawed, Rosaldo initially suggested that such converts were simply turning to fantasies of heaven to deny death's reality. What he wrote of anger, though, helped me acknowledge my own. Much later, for me as for him, raw experience poured into what I was writing, as I

sought to untangle my own responses, while sensing how powerfully our culture shapes them.

More than a year after Heinz died, often overcome by emotional storms and bouts of pneumonia, I was asked to speak
at the New York Psychoanalytic Society. Some of its members,
intrigued by what I'd written in *Adam, Eve, and the Serpent*
about sexuality and politics, invited me to speak at their annual meeting. But the topic they chose for their next meeting
was "rage, power, and aggression." Startled, at first I refused;
how could I speak to *that*? But on reflection, I realized that
Heinz's death compelled me to contend with the ways that our
culture interprets—and represses—rage and aggression. Realizing, ruefully, that I was, indeed, qualified, I felt that speaking about rage might help gain some sorely needed perspective,
and so I dived in.

Now, as I began to reread familiar biblical stories, I became
much more aware that while Ilongot culture celebrates anger,
even intentional murder, done "for cause," our culture vilifies it.
I was startled to see that the first story in *Genesis* that mentions
human anger, for example, tells how the Lord himself warns
Cain, violently jealous of his brother, Abel, to master rage, lest
it overpower him. When Cain's anger boils over and he mur-
ders his brother, he barely escapes being killed himself, and,
stigmatized, suffers punishment for the rest of his life. Biblical
stories show that those who grieve the dead—bereaved mothers
and fathers, brothers and sisters—are expected to respond not
with anger but with sadness, putting ashes on their heads, tearing their own clothes—in effect, inflicting pain on themselves, in
practices that anthropologists call self-mortification (literally,
"killing oneself"). For from the start—the biblical story of Adam

and Eve—the Bible interprets death, especially death through illness, war, or accident, as punishment for sin.

What surprised me was to see that biblical stories reserve anger, especially righteous anger that motivates killing, as the special prerogative of the Lord himself. The Bible's Exodus stories, for example, praise the Lord for destroying the entire Egyptian army "in his fury." Later, when the Lord's "anger burns hot" against his own people, he resolves to kill them, too. Although initially Moses pleads with the Lord to relent, when Moses sees his people worshipping a Canaanite god, his own "anger burns hot" on the Lord's behalf. Summoning the Levites, he shouts out orders: "Thus says the Lord, the God of Israel: 'Put your sword on your side, each of you! Go back and forth . . . throughout the camp, and each of you, kill your brother, your friend, and your neighbor.'" After the Levites go on a rampage through the camp and mercilessly slaughter three thousand of their own people, Moses praises them for having "served the Lord." Then he announces that *since each one of them has killed his own brothers and sons,* "you have . . . brought a blessing upon yourselves this day."

Yet even these early biblical stories I found hint that the people who told them felt conflicted, as I did, about acknowledging anger. Another story, for example, tells how "the Lord's anger was kindled against Israel, and he incited King David" to take a census in order to initiate taxes and conscript men into the army—an innovation that intensely angers many people, including the storyteller. But he ends this story with a strange contradiction: even though *the Lord himself initiated the census, the Lord harshly punishes David for having done it,* sending an avenging angel to destroy Jerusalem and all its inhabitants, relenting only after David humbly repents, the angel having killed seventy thousand Israelites!

Some anonymous writer, however, obviously uncomfortable with this story, wrote a second version, inserting Satan into the story to make it more consistent. This second version, also in the Bible, says that *Satan* incited David's evil act, and that after "*Satan* opposed Israel, and incited David to count the people . . . *God* was displeased with this thing, and struck Israel." This revised version concludes by telling how God sends his avenging angel to punish the king, killing seventy thousand people. But as the angel raises his sword to destroy Jerusalem, David does elaborate penance, wearing sackcloth and offering lavish atonement sacrifices, until "the Lord took note, and relented . . . and said to the angel, 'Enough! Stay your hand . . .' and the angel put his sword back into its sheath," canceling further slaughter.

Comparing the two versions, I felt that perhaps I could understand why the second writer revised the story. For even though talk of being "angry at God" sounded to me like nonsense, I felt it would be a relief, when grieving and raging, to have *someone* to blame. So, too, these storytellers chose not to blame God for disaster, and blamed instead a member of his heavenly court, whom they called "the *satan*," imagining him as a malicious trickster who throws obstacles into one's path, sometimes hidden like land mines, to lure his targets toward danger and death.

So, I thought, with some irony, why not blame Satan, rather than reflexively blaming myself, or allowing anyone to blame those who died? For me this started almost as a joke, or, rather, as a way of deflecting anger, since I thought of Satan, if at all, as a kind of throwaway figure, two horns and a tail scrawled onto a cartoon, or a bogeyman that only children and superstitious people feared. Yet now I realized that for millennia, people had bushwhacked through rough emotional terrain partly by envisioning Satan—or, in the case of those who worshipped the traditional Greek gods, the gods themselves—as invisible antagonists.

Recalling that a vision of Satan, menacing and dangerous, had appeared in my dream the night before our son's open-heart surgery, I realized that although I didn't *believe in* him, the figure often called "the old enemy" nevertheless lived in my imagination, shaped by ancient cultural traditions, catalyzed by crisis. And although at the time I did not practice prayer, in that dream I'd spoken the words "Jesus Christ," involuntarily crying out a powerful name to ward off a threatening presence, as Christians have done for thousands of years. So even if Satan is a figment of the imagination, he's the shape imagination has given to some of our most immediate experiences—in my case, fear of our child's death, and desperate hope.

I recalled that what triggered that dream was having heard, that afternoon, a choir singing the famous hymn in which Martin Luther pictures God as a mighty fortress, a refuge in time of war. For this hymn goes on to warn that "still our ancient foe doth seek to work us woe / His power and craft are great / And armed with cruel hate, on earth is not his equal." When Luther wrote this, he took his cues from the New Testament's stories of Jesus's conflicts with the devil—one of countless ways in which Christians and Muslims have adapted and transformed stories of Satan for thousands of years. Such stories acknowledge the power that death holds over all of us, but they also speak of hope for reprieve, even from a God whom many no longer believe in but who may, nevertheless, live in our unconscious, when we cry out "Oh, my God!"

During those dark, nameless days and months, like many people feeling overwhelmed, I did think of Job. Surely only a woman who'd failed as mother and wife would see both her child and husband die. Could this be punishment for some unknown, unacknowledged sin? Struggling to untangle such messy emotions, I sensed how unconsciously I'd absorbed cultural messages from those ancient traditions, long after my family had given up Christianity. For when those biblical stories turn grief away from anger, they turn it toward guilt. For me, then, as for many others, when grieving, guilt crashed in with harsh and dissonant chords that nearly drowned out anger. Job's problem—acknowledging only one God, while insisting that he's both good and just—is that when something goes wrong, there's no one to blame but yourself.

Much as I'd resisted Palo Alto's suburban cocoon, growing up there had allowed me to assume that disasters wouldn't happen to people like ourselves—not, at least, to those who hadn't done something dreadfully wrong. Wasn't there some kind of moral system in the universe, some afterimage of an ancient God whom we could count on to keep track of what's fair? Especially after the unimaginable had happened, the death of our child? Sufferings that others endured, many much worse, since they were intentionally inflicted, like those of countless people whose lives were stolen, ravaged, and destroyed by slavery and racial hatred, and like the millions slaughtered or damaged in the Nazi death camps and countless other genocides, had so far remained at some distance and failed to penetrate my naivete.

Yet it wasn't only the smugness of suburban America that kept the sufferings of others at a distance. Even the storyteller who wrote Job's story thousands of years ago apparently objected to the earliest version of that ancient folktale—the version that tells only of a man who suffers without complaint, never losing his trust in God. As I reread that ancient story now, it seemed to break open like a pomegranate, bloodred on the inside, showing how schizophrenic it is, or, if you like, how brilliantly complex. For what we call "the *Book of Job*," as if it were a single book, actually stitches together what look like two distinctly different writings. Whoever wrote the version we now have in the Bible apparently began by telling only the first part of an ancient folktale, then split it into two parts, placing the second part at the end. Spliced into the middle, he added his own voice—the voice of an anguished, angry poet, who speaks for countless people devastated by war, driven as exiles into poverty, who'd seen their children die and buried them while living as refugees scrambling for scraps of their previous lives. This poet outrageously protests—even mocks—the folktale's simple moralism, while claiming to give voice to Job's anguish.

So I felt driven to probe into his story. The folktale, then, goes like this: First the *satan*, a member of God's heavenly court, appears before God to question Job's piety, insinuating that his loyalty to God depends only on his good fortune. Apparently stung by this challenge, the Lord then allows the *satan* to test Job. First, enemy soldiers kill Job's servants and steal his oxen and donkeys; then "fire from God" falls from heaven and burns up his flocks of sheep; finally, his oldest son's house collapses, crushing to death all ten of his sons and daughters. And even after the *satan* goes further, inflicting him with horrible sores all over his body, Job maintains his simple faith in God. While mourning his dead children, he never speaks a word against God—or so says the folktale that opens his story.

The *Book of Job* ends with the second half of this moralistic folktale: the Lord rewards Job's patience by giving him back "twice as much as he had before"—fourteen thousand sheep, six thousand camels, a thousand yoke of oxen, a thousand donkeys, and seven more sons and three beautiful daughters. By adding this "happy ending," the storyteller reassures his hearers that no matter what happens, "God's in his heaven; all's right with the world," or will be—just as the Colorado policeman wanted to tell me when delivering news that my husband was dead.

But as the third chapter starts, the *poet's* Job first opens his mouth, cursing the day he was born, crying out that he wishes he were dead. This Job tears open the tension hidden in Israel's claim that there is only one, all-powerful God; for if so, then God himself creates all the horrors of the world, and hope for divine justice is futile. When Job's friends come to console him, they wrap themselves in traditional pieties, telling Job that although he *looks* like an upright man, he must have done something wrong, likely in secret; otherwise, surely he would not suffer like this. But Job insists that although he isn't perfect, he's done nothing to deserve such huge catastrophes. Now he wants to subpoena God—demand that the Lord himself appear in court and admit that Job is telling the truth. But when he fails to bring his divine tormentor to justice, Job cries out that his tormentor is none other than God himself: "He has torn me apart in his wrath, and hated me; he has gnashed his teeth at me," hunting Job down to destroy him. *"If it is not he, then who is it?"*

To answer that question—and deflect blame from God—later generations would invent the figure of Satan. But the poet leaves Satan out, picturing the Lord himself as a terrifying figure who arrives in a whirlwind. Instead of answering Job's questions, the Lord challenges him, sarcastically demanding that he answer to *him*: "Who is this who darkens understanding with ignorant words? . . . Where were you when I laid the foundations of the earth? Tell me—surely you know!" This ferocious apparition dares Job to "behold Behemoth, whom I made as I made you," the "first of the great acts of God," along with Leviathan—the two mythological monsters of Jewish legend who embody chaos, danger, and the raging, devouring sea. Now Job confronts a vision of the universe radically different from *Genesis*'s orderly creation: a world on fire, like a monstrous being exploding with primal energy that "not even the gods dare challenge," since "terror dances before it." That's the kind of vision in which the Greeks, like many others, envisioned the powers of their capricious gods, givers of life and death—powers that contemporary culture has sought to domesticate as "forces of nature."

Greeks who worshipped such gods had no need for Satan, since their prophets never claimed that the gods were unequivocally good. Poets like Homer told how they might favor or kill you, depending on their changing moods. Apollo, who rides with the sun, bringing light and glory, might suddenly turn and shoot his bow, sending deadly plague; Aphrodite, who graced Helen of Troy with astonishing beauty, turns harsh and hostile the moment Helen questions her orders, threatening to abandon her former favorite to her enemies' revenge. Such traditions, from Homer's *Iliad* to the story of Job, speak of powerful forces, variously seen as natural or divine, bringing wonder and terror, acting like the sunlight and rain that sustain our lives, yet sometimes turn into drought, lightning, and deadly floods.

Why, then, do disasters still shock and surprise us? As I see it, the priests who arranged the present composition of the Hebrew Bible, starting with the first creation story, effectively set up what philosophers call "the problem of evil." For if we believe that an all-powerful God created a "very good" world, what happened to it? While the Buddha declared as his first noble truth that "all life is suffering," Jewish and Christian theologians, on the contrary, speak of "the problem of suffering," as if suffering and death were not intrinsic elements of nature but alien intruders on an originally perfect creation. And although Western culture offers a range of conflicting traditions, from Homer's *Iliad* to the poem of Job, most biblical stories insist that the divine source is good—that, in Einstein's witty phrase, "The Lord may be subtle, but he is not malicious." Maybe we need to believe that: even the *Book of Job*, in its present form, ends with the folktale's happy ending. So we're stuck with this problem, and left with no answers.

Months after Heinz's death, when I was able to sleep at night, sometimes for minutes, sometimes an hour or more, I'd often spend them with him in dreams, and wake to the shock of his absence. Sometimes, though, in a dream, I'd run to embrace him, only to have him turn away, inexplicably indifferent, as he'd never done in life. The following spring, I panicked. What to do? Going back to where *that* happened felt impossible. Where, then, to go? Finally I realized that even going to the other side of the world would make no difference; the grief would be right there with us. So I booked our tickets for Colorado. Holding David in a baby carrier, and Sarah by the hand, dreading the moment of arrival, I finally stepped off the airplane into the small mountain airport, surprised, at that moment, to feel some slight relief. The vast forests and surrounding mountains seemed to place our situation into a far greater perspective.

That July, on the first anniversary of his death, I drove out to the monastery. Seated with two monks on a wooden bench in that simple brick chapel, I began to meditate, hoping, even expecting, that the day might bring some consolation. Instead, the opposite happened. When I closed my eyes, what I first saw was that familiar tape loop, visualizing him starting to descend down the path on Pyramid Peak, then suddenly falling, falling fast, toward the rocks below. That's where the tape always had stopped abruptly and started over. For a year I'd seen him slip and fall, over and over, an endless cycle.

This time it changed. As the silence enveloped us, the meditation went deeper, supported by the presence of the monks engaged in prayer. The same scene appeared, but this time it did not stop. Instead, to my shock, I saw him dash against the rocks that shattered his body, as rivers of blood gushed forth, more blood than I'd ever imagined could come from one person. Transfixed with horror, I watched, sitting entirely still, uttering no sound. I had the distinct impression—and still do—that somehow I'd actually seen it happen but had blocked it out of consciousness until that moment. When we finally emerged, I walked unsteadily out of the darkened chapel into startling sunlight, and drove home.

That evening, our home was filled with friends from town, close friends among the physicists, and Father Joseph from the monastery. When I'd first invited him, he gently explained that he could not come, having taking the vow that required him to stay at the monastery. "But Joseph," I protested, "even Jesus went to dinner parties!" After consulting with his spiritual director, he did come to join us, wearing jeans and a plaid work shirt. Feeling strange at what I'd seemed to have seen, I was grateful to be surrounded with friends that evening. A week later, I talked with a grief counselor, who explained that when someone dies in an accident and survivors cannot see the body, they do not fully comprehend that the person has died until they completely visualize what happened. Now, involuntarily, that had happened. But, I told her, the only thing about that experience that wasn't realistic was how much blood I saw. "That's what happens in a real accident," she replied.

How to go on? Viktor Frankl, in a far more drastic situation, wrote that when our lives turn out different from what we expect, we have to do "what life expects of us":

> We needed to stop asking about the meaning of life, and instead think of ourselves as those who are being questioned by life—daily and hourly. . . . Life ultimately means taking the responsibility to find the right answer to its problems, and to fulfill the tasks which it constantly sets for each individual.

What I had to do next, since my salary alone could not pay the mortgage for our apartment in New York, was to put it on the market and take the children to live in Princeton, since now I'd be supporting the three of us alone, and, I hoped, somehow, find the resources to forge a new life.

The next January, in 1989, the New York Academy of Sciences' annual dinner was to be held at the Museum of Natural History. Especially since Heinz would not be there, his colleagues expected me to come. A year earlier, he had invited his respected senior colleague, the physicist Freeman Dyson, to be the speaker. Walking alone to that dinner, braced against an icy wind on a winter night, felt nearly impossible; crying uncontrollably, I almost turned back home. But when I finally arrived, I was relieved to be seated next to the speaker, having deeply appreciated his kindness, as the father of six children, during Mark's illness. As we talked over dinner, he suggested that I take a year off from teaching and come as a visitor to the Institute for Advanced Study. Since often I felt exhausted, depleted of the energy that teaching requires, I was grateful for his suggestion, but since membership in the Institute is a privilege that its faculty offers on the basis of prospective research, I didn't want to be there simply because kind friends might suggest it. So I applied to the Institute's School of Historical Studies, proposing as my project the research that would lead to my book *The Origin of Satan*.

The next August, after clearing out our home and listing it for sale, I put everything in storage, piled up boxes full of books and financial records, and moved with the children into the small, simple apartment that the institute assigned to us on Einstein Drive. We lived opposite an identical apartment occupied by a family from Tel Aviv, whose children, Tamar and Daniel, were the same age as Sarah and David. From there we could walk to Crossroads Nursery School, a comfortable space with outdoor playgrounds, where Sarah and David could join children of other institute members to swing, climb the slides and go down, or play with trucks in the sandbox, speaking Chinese, Spanish, Hebrew, French, Russian, and a variety of languages I couldn't identify. On weekday mornings, after walking there with the children, grateful for the time, I'd carry two strong cups of coffee to a bare office overlooking fields and trees. At the time, I jokingly thought of this peaceful refuge as a much-needed mental hospital, a private sanatorium, where I hoped that writing might help clarify the noisy cacophony swirling through me.

Sitting there at a wooden desk, facing empty pages and a blank computer screen, I was stopped. How had I ever imagined that I could engage in creative work again? A practical friend, a writer himself, said, "Why not skip the academic stuff, and write about what you're dealing with—write about grief?" "I don't want to write about grief—what, go on talk shows and act like some kind of *expert*? I hate grief—I just want to get through it!" What he suggested sounded blinding and futile, like staring into the sun—or into a black hole. Besides, anything written with passion, "academic" or otherwise, inevitably engages whatever challenges we're confronting.

Back, then, to Satan. How to start? I began exploring a handful of stories in the Hebrew Bible, in apocryphal Jewish sources, in the Dead Sea Scrolls, and in writings of Jesus's followers, to see how, some two thousand years ago, various people had spun the figure of Satan out of their own conflict and pain. How, then, did this figure of Satan originate? Who invented him, and why? Asking these questions allowed me to acknowledge emotions that made no rational sense; and this seemed an innocuous, perhaps therapeutic, way of dealing with them.

What first surprised me was to see that Satan does not appear in the Hebrew Bible—not, at least, as Christians and Muslims know him, as an evil supernatural power. Christians who identify the snake in Paradise as Satan actually are projecting a far more recent invention into that ancient story, since the *Genesis* folktale pictures the serpent only as a cunning, talking snake, perhaps a stand-in for the humans' inner voice. A handful of stories in the Hebrew Bible do speak of a supernatural character they call "the *satan*"—a name that characterizes his role as "adversary," but in these stories he acts more like a storytelling device than a dangerous enemy. As in the story of Job, his presence often marks misfortune, a setback, or a twist in the plot. But before the first century CE, groups of dissident Jews, including Jesus's followers, began to turn this rather unpleasant angel into the far more powerful, malevolent figure whom Christians and Muslims see as personifying evil, making war on God and humankind alike.

Reading a book by Jeffrey Burton Russell, who has written five books on the devil and his origin, I was stopped by one sentence: "The figure of Satan has nothing to do with social history." *Impossible!* I thought; that's obviously wrong. People who take Satan seriously, whether thousands of years ago or today, aren't simply imagining ethereal spirits clashing in the stratosphere. Anyone who says, for example, that "Satan is trying to take over this country," has in mind *certain people* right here on the ground, seen as Satan's agents—and likely could give you names and addresses!

That misguided sentence spurred me to write what I privately—and ironically—called "the social history of Satan." How, after all, could an imaginary being have a social history?

But I'd begun to see that Satan does—and wanted to track it down. Why were Christians writing about Satan? How do they associate him with certain people, and who are those people? What *practical* difference does it make to put Satan into a story?

I found a clue in the famous "Scroll of the War of the Sons of Light against the Sons of Darkness," discovered in 1947 in Israel among the Dead Sea Scrolls, a sacred library hidden in caves apparently by the strict sect of Jews often called Essenes, who'd withdrawn from ordinary Jewish society to protest Rome's occupation of Israel. Whoever wrote this scroll warns the "holy ones," as "sons of light," to prepare to fight on the side of the angels to destroy "the sons of darkness," allies of the Evil One, a.k.a. Satan, Prince of Darkness. The *Book of Jubilees* also calls him *Mastema*, perhaps his most appropriate name: "hatred."

The author of the War Scroll envisions God contending against Satan, and sees the human world similarly divided. Thus members of the desert community see themselves fighting against outsiders, including uninitiated Jews who, they charge, have gone over to the dark side and unwittingly serve Satan. Anyone entering this sacred community would have to swear to love and defend his fellow "holy ones," and "to hate the sons of darkness"—not only the hated Romans, but also all Jews who cooperate with the Roman occupation. Were these devout sectarians expecting God to send an army of angels to destroy Rome by divine power, or were they actually stockpiling weapons to fight? We can't know for sure; but since Roman military leaders assumed that they were preparing for war, battalions of Roman soldiers besieged their fortified camp near the Dead Sea in 70 CE, and slaughtered everyone they found there.

Since Jesus of Nazareth, a contemporary of the Essenes,

shared a similar vision, his earliest followers also saw themselves caught in conflict between God's spirit and Satan. Who, then, did they see as God's people, and who as Satan's? When first asking this question, I thought the answer was obvious: they'd identify Jesus and his disciples—and, by extension, themselves— with God's spirit; and they'd see "Satan's people" as the Jewish leaders who opposed and arrested Jesus, and the Romans who sentenced and crucified him.

But I was wrong—and astonished. When I began to reread the gospels stories, I was surprised to see that they *never* blame the Romans for killing Jesus. Instead, they blame only the *Jewish* enemies of Jesus—first of all, Judas Iscariot, whose name, in Greek, connotes "Jew" (*Ioudas*); then they blame the chief priest and the Jewish council, who, Mark says, sentenced Jesus to death. Matthew's gospel goes so far as to blame "all the people," and John's gospel accuses "the Jews"—as if Jesus weren't Jewish himself!

But why, I wondered, would Jewish writers indict only Jews, even if some did play a role in Jesus's arrest, while exempting the Romans, who, as all the evidence indicates, crucified Jesus on charges of inciting revolution against Rome? After struggling with this question, I began to untangle a convoluted story, which I describe in *The Origin of Satan*. Here I can only quickly sketch how, having started out investigating Satan, I was shocked—and dismayed—to have stumbled unexpectedly onto the origins of Christian anti-Judaism, which later ignited into Christian anti-Semitism. Most simply put, Jesus's earliest followers spun the story as they did because they were terrified of being arrested and killed themselves.

The earliest gospel writer, whom we call Mark, likely had

lived through some forty years of violent clashes between Roman soldiers and Jewish militants fighting to regain their independence from Rome. During those tumultuous years, Jesus of Nazareth was only one of thousands of Jews whom Roman soldiers crucified on charges of inciting revolution. The magistrates who ordered those crucifixions would have felt their suspicions fully justified in 66 CE, when Jewish revolutionaries broke into open war, fighting "in the name of God and our common liberty," as American revolutionaries would do nearly two thousand years later. But unlike the American Revolution, the Jewish revolution failed. After four years of ferocious fighting, during which some sixty thousand Roman soldiers besieged, starved, and pillaged Jerusalem, they finally attacked the Jerusalem Temple, where the militants had barricaded themselves to fight a desperate last stand. Then the Roman commander proclaimed victory and ordered his soldiers to plunder, desecrate, and tear down the temple, and set fire to its remains, reducing the sacred center of the city to an enormous heap of charred rubble.

Even after the war, Roman officers continued to suspect Jews of inciting revolution, including followers of Jesus, who remained doggedly loyal to their dead leader, convicted and executed for sedition. Others, too, were targeted and killed—Peter, caught, tortured, and crucified; Paul, arrested, often put on trial, horribly whipped, and finally beheaded; and Jesus's own brother, James, lynched by a mob near the Jerusalem Temple.

Acutely aware of the danger, Mark and the others chose to narrate Jesus's death in ways that emphasize his innocence—and their own. When I realized the situation in which they were writing, I began to understand why they'd spun their stories defensively, shifting the blame for his crucifixion onto certain

Jewish leaders. Mark goes so far as to suggest that chief priests invented the charge of sedition to trick the Romans into crucifying Jesus, and that Pilate, the Roman governor, recognized Jesus's innocence. As Mark tells it, Pilate worked hard to save Jesus's life, rejecting the priests' accusations and defending him from a hostile crowd of Jews shouting for crucifixion, until finally, still unconvinced of Jesus's guilt, he gave in to placate the mob.

Everything we know of Roman history shows that this story is extremely unlikely, since it contradicts everything that Pilate's contemporaries say about him and about Roman policies toward Jews accused of sedition. But the story stuck—and still holds sway in the gospel accounts. Yet when spinning the story this way, Mark apparently didn't intend to denigrate his fellow Jews so much as to save his own life, and those of others loyal to Jesus.

While discovering what happened, though, I realized that whatever the gospel writers had in mind, or didn't, matters less than the unintended consequences. Mark's successors added even more incendiary details to his story; Matthew's gospel, as noted, pictures "the whole nation" of Jews calling down a blood curse on themselves, while shouting for Jesus's death: "His blood be upon us, and upon our children." And John's gospel, written perhaps a decade later, pictures Jesus himself denouncing "the Jews" in first-century hate speech, as if he weren't one of them: "You are of your father, the devil . . . and he was a liar and murderer from the beginning!"

Over two hundred years later, as Constantine and his successors began to shift imperial policies toward what they saw as Christian values, "Christian prejudices against the Jews became legal disabilities"; now, for example, Christian legal codes decreed that converting someone to Judaism was a crime punishable by death. Christian bishops today revered as saints, including Saint Augustine, bishop of Hippo, and Saint Athanasius, bishop of Alexandria, seized on gospel accounts of Jesus's death to demonize Jews as "Christ killers"—guilty not only of murder, but even of the recently invented crime of deicide, "killing God." Such traditions, sometimes hidden, often exposed, have set off a long and horrific history of pogroms, lynching, legal restrictions, even genocide—first against Jews and dissident Christians called heretics, then against "infidels," and, more recently, against tribal people branded as "Satan worshippers."

All of this came to me as a tremendous shock. What seemed so innocuous when I started—investigating an imaginary angel gone rogue—suddenly jolted me back into the real world. Even more, this research opened up an ominous undercurrent in Christian tradition—one with very real, and terrible, consequences. When I spoke about this with a friend raised Catholic, she objected: "But isn't Christianity all about love?" At its best, of course, it is, but not without an undercurrent of hate.

What struck me, too, is that the Christian stories that Renato Rosaldo dismissed as mere "solutions of the imagination" could evoke destruction as real and as horrific as the headhunters' rage, and likely far more so. Throughout two thousand years of Christian history, the use of these stories in war, especially by Christians and Muslims, has resulted in countless people killed "in the name of God." People who interpret human conflict in terms of good against evil, God against Satan, obviously find it much easier to kill those they identify as evil—even to insist that killing them is morally necessary.

But when we take one step further, we can see that the head-hunters' ritual is no less a "solution of the imagination." For how could anyone imagine that tossing away a head could "carry his anger," unless he'd been nurtured in the (imaginative) traditions of a culture that taught him that? How could the political and military leaders of any nation today engage in genocide unless deeply felt traditions persuaded them that "ethnic cleansing" could "purify" a group "polluted" by people they see as alien? Only imagination, apparently, can evoke the visceral, powerful responses required to wage war, incite terrorism and acts of violence, whether triggered by fear, paranoia, or patriotic emotion. No wonder that all over the world, throughout human history, tribes and peoples have relied on religious traditions—rituals, music, narratives—to arouse the passions that prove so useful, even indispensable, in war.

This doesn't mean, though, what people who hate religion often say—that religion simply *causes* violence, pogroms, and war, which may be triggered by all kinds of conflict. What it *does* mean, as we've seen, is that simplistic scenarios of good against evil encourage people to interpret conflict as nonnegotiable. Nor does it support the opposite, equally superficial claim that "there's no such thing as evil." As I see it, acts of violence, especially against defenseless people, are unquestionably evil. But reflecting on stories of Satan has led me to avoid using the term "evil" to characterize entire groups of people, or even individuals, and to apply the term instead to specific *acts*.

Above all, exploring stories of Satan shows that *what we imagine* is enormously consequential. Are "solutions of the imagination" nothing but ways to deny reality, as Renato Rosaldo initially suggested? No doubt that's one way to use them.

But having been unable to deny reality, even when I most wanted to, I'm convinced that we cannot interpret our own experience, much less that of our culture, without simultaneously engaging *both* imagination and rationality. So far, we've been looking at negative consequences of religious traditions, crucial for understanding their impact on Western history. But I've come to see that there are other aspects of these complex cultural traditions—even stories about Satan—that also may help people *cope* with reality; may even offer practical ways to confront it.

CHAPTER 7

Wrestling with the Devil

Mark and Heinz Pagels, in Castle Creek, Colorado.

At three A.M., alone in the dark, endless hours before dawn, I turned to where for so long he'd slept, as we'd closed each day comfortably intertwined, and awakened every morning to each other's rhythms. Now, reaching toward him, I felt only crumpled sheets and empty space, his absence still somehow a shock, every time. Dark outside, still dark, a low hum of traffic seared by an ambulance siren; after three or four more hours, I might hear a clatter of garbage cans. Already it's been so long; weeks, months, even years. Why did I feel as if he'd just fallen, or even as if it hadn't happened yet, could somehow be stopped, turned back?

Shaking with tears as memories flooded back, I realized how many of them had vanished a year after Mark died, when Heinz's death crashed over us like a tsunami. Even as the wave receded, I was living in a world of raw absence, shock, dumb grief. And the same questions tumbled back, over and over. How could *that* have happened—just as we'd begun to imagine that we might be able to survive the death of our child? Hadn't we paid our dues, and more? How to go on, without drowning in despair?

I'd seen what happened to Heinz's mother. Having anticipated that we would hold each other close after these losses, since now we lived nearby, I was disappointed; instead, she withdrew, her lips firmly closed, stoically silent. What surprised and grieved me even more was that she scarcely could bear to see me and the children; apparently our presence recalled too sharply the deaths of her son and grandson. Devastated, as if irreparably broken, this strong woman fell ill, lingering for months before she died. Heinz's brother, her older son, was with her, but he neither notified us nor invited us to her funeral, if he'd arranged one; we never heard from him. I realized that she may have requested that.

Every morning, before school, I'd make the effort to get up, wake the children, look for matching socks and sort out clothes to help them get dressed, make breakfast, do whatever had to be done; but on many dark mornings even that felt impossible. Then there were days that hit with the sharpness of new grief, which I longed to dodge, or at least postpone. So about a year and a half after Heinz died, when I was invited to the University of Texas, I agreed to speak on the anniversary of Mark's death, hoping that the intense engagement of giving a talk might help me get through a day that, left open, could smack me down like a tidal wave, sobbing, gasping for breath.

At the airport in Austin, I was met by a young couple who hugged me as if we were close friends and invited me to their home for lunch. As they talked familiarly of Heinz and Mark, I realized that they'd been in our New York apartment. Somehow I recognized them, but how? Who were they? Had he been one of Heinz's graduate students in physics? After a couple of hours, when his wife spoke of what happened the day that Mark died, suddenly I remembered. She'd been a student of mine at Barnard, who, after taking my class, chose to become a historian of religion herself, a scholar of Tibetan Buddhism. In January of her senior year, needing to supplement college expenses, she and her boyfriend, now her husband, had come to live in a room in our apartment while they helped care for the children on weekends. They'd been living with us for months when Mark died in April, and for months after that—and I hadn't recognized them!

Astonished, I remembered what the emergency room doctor had told me, when he saw me a few days after Heinz died with boils all over my body: post-traumatic stress can obliterate memory. Yet blocked memories return, often in fragments. When Mark died, we felt that the worst we'd ever imagined had happened; how, then, had this unimaginable loss shattered our lives a second time?

After I returned from Austin, these questions recurred. I was startled to realize that somehow I still wanted to believe that we live in a morally ordered universe, in which someone, or something—God or nature?—would keep track of what's fair. Was this a relic of Western cultural tradition that moralizes history, like those old Bible stories I'd heard, that suggest that doing good ensures well being and doing wrong brings disaster? The biblical story of Sodom, for example, in which a volcano erupts and destroys two cities, concludes that the Lord "rained fire from heaven, and destroyed those cities . . . and all their inhabitants" because "the men of Sodom, young and old, all of them, down to the last man" were evil. No mention of women and children, I noted; were they only collateral damage? Another Bible story, noting that King David and Bathsheba's first son died young, explains that "the Lord struck the child . . . and it died," to punish their illicit sexual connection.

Now, working hard to stay steady, or seem to, I could no longer afford to look through a lens that heaps guilt upon grief. Although I wasn't a traditional believer and didn't take such

stories literally, somehow their premises had shaped my unconscious assumptions. Now I had to divest myself of the illusion that we *deserved* what had happened; believing it would
have crushed us. Instead, I turned again to what Heinz often
had said about chaos theory and randomness, and I shifted
more toward his understanding of nature. Now I was living in a
world where volcanoes erupt because that's what volcanoes do,
regardless of whether anyone in their path is good or evil, and
in which children often die young, for no reason we can find.

Two years later, when members of the Episcopal church in
Aspen asked me to come back and give a sermon there, at first
I said, "No, thank you; I'm not a preacher." I didn't say that the
sight of Heinz's casket, placed in front of that altar, was indelibly imprinted in my memory. But on second thought, I agreed.
I *did* want to speak there—to speak *against* the facile comfort
that churches often dole out like Kleenex. So the next summer,
voice breaking with emotion, I spoke what emerged from internal turmoil, contrasting two stories that helped me find words.
For while scholars of literature like to say that we use stories
to "think with," we also use them to "feel with"—that is, to find
words for what otherwise we could not say.

On that Sunday morning I contrasted Job's story—Job loses
everything, then gets it all back—with the story in Mark's gospel. For while Jesus of Nazareth and his followers likely knew
Job's story, Mark's account of Jesus doesn't end that way. Mark
opens by claiming to announce "good news of Jesus, Messiah,
Son of God," but the story he tells ends in disaster, when a posse
of armed men suddenly capture and arrest Jesus at night, as his
followers scatter and run. The original version of Mark's gospel says that after his captors amused themselves by mocking

and torturing Jesus, they handed him over to the Roman governor. Accused of igniting revolution, although innocent, he was mocked, spat on, and beaten before enduring a cruelly slow and humiliating public execution. In the original version that Mark wrote, Jesus, crucified in agony, cries out, "My God, my God, why have you abandoned me?" then "let[s] out a loud cry" and dies.

Similar things have happened, of course, to countless others, and still do. And in Mark's original version, as so often in stories we hear today, no angel appears, no miracle intervenes. Instead, after telling how Roman soldiers crucified Jesus, this story ends with an abrupt, disturbing scene at the grave site, in which Jesus's women followers, having come to tend his body, find it missing. This version ends as the women, hearing a young man say that they'll see Jesus alive again, are so shocked and frightened that they "went out and fled . . . and said nothing to anyone, because they were terrified."

When I first read that version, I wondered, How could Mark possibly claim to publish "good news" when his story ends in desolation and terror? In graduate school, I learned that some of Mark's earliest readers had asked similar questions, and some decided that he *couldn't* have meant to end that way; he must have left his story unfinished. Editors of contemporary Bibles apparently agree: nearly every Bible published today includes *another* ending that some other writer added to Mark's original narrative.

So far as we can tell, this is what happened: Someone among Mark's early readers, wanting the gospel to end on a more positive note, wrote a *second* ending, adding several episodes to mitigate that awful final scene. This second ending says that after his burial, "Jesus first appeared to Mary Magdalene," but when she told the disciples, "they would not believe it." Then Jesus appeared to two others "in another form," but none of the disciples believed that either. Finally he shocked them by appearing a third time, while they were at dinner, and scolded them for refusing to believe that he'd come back to life. This second ending, now included in virtually all Bibles, concludes as Jesus, triumphant, "was taken up into heaven, and sat down at the right hand of God," while his disciples, filled with the holy spirit, "went out and proclaimed the good news everywhere."

Rereading this after Heinz's death, I began to note how, when the writers we call Matthew and Luke set out to revise Mark's narrative, each piled on even more elaborate resurrection stories, obviously writing them to refute what skeptics were saying. Luke suggests that what "terrified" the women was seeing *two* men in dazzling clothes—angels, apparently—suddenly appear in the empty grave, announcing that Jesus was alive. Then Luke adds that Jesus appeared to two disciples on the road to Emmaus, just as the others were hearing that "the Lord actually *has* risen, and appeared to Peter!" Luke agrees that at first the disciples themselves didn't believe it, and were "astonished and terrified, and thought they were seeing a ghost" when Jesus suddenly "stood there among them, and greeted them." To dispel their shock and disbelief, Jesus showed them his wounds, saying, "Touch me and see; for a ghost does not have flesh and bones, as you see that I have." But, Luke adds, since they still were "disbelieving and wondering," Jesus asked for something to eat, and ate fish in front of them, to prove that he was "not a ghost!" Like Mark's second ending, Luke's account concludes as Jesus ascends into heaven, promising to send "power from on high," as his disciples "rejoice with great joy."

Matthew, like Luke, writing independently about ten years after Mark, adds a whole chapter to counter rumors that Jesus's followers stole his body to fake a resurrection. As Matthew tells it, after Jewish authorities alerted Pilate to this danger, the governor ordered soldiers to secure the grave with a huge stone, and stationed guards to keep watch. But suddenly "there was a great earthquake, and an angel of the Lord descended from heaven . . . rolled away the stone and sat on it," as the terrified soldiers fell to the ground "like dead men." Matthew admits that the women ran away, but not, he insists, because they were shocked into silence. Instead, he says that they "ran in fear and great joy, to tell his disciples." Then, even before they departed, Matthew says, Jesus appeared to the women, who ran toward him and "held on to his feet and worshipped him." Here, too, the point is clear: to show that he was physically present, not a ghost. In Matthew's final scene, "the eleven," the male disciples, too, see Jesus alive (although, oddly, Matthew notes that even then "some doubted"). Now ready to begin his reign, Jesus proclaims that now, in heaven, God has given him "all authority, on heaven and on earth!"

Troubling as others found Mark's original version, I preferred it. What he wrote sounded more like the world in which we live. For when he began to write, he faced a challenge that I, like so many of us, could understand: how to hold on to hope when confronting what looks like disaster. His challenge, of course, was particularly dramatic. The Greek philosopher Celsus, who despised Christians, spoke for many outsiders who mocked their grandiose claims. How, Celsus asked, could anyone possibly believe that Jesus of Nazareth, who'd died decades earlier, not only *was*, but still *is*, God's Messiah, divinely chosen to rule the whole world? If Jesus really *were* God's son, how could his followers have abandoned him and gone into hiding, while enemy soldiers seized and killed him as a common criminal? And how could hope survive the war, when Jesus's followers—and his whole people—had endured what, in Mark's narrative, Jesus calls "such suffering as has not been seen from the beginning of creation until now, no, and never will be"?

Like many other Jews who lived through that war, and a handful of others still loyal to Jesus, Mark apparently felt that the old script—*things turn out well for the righteous, badly for evildoers*—no longer worked. Few of his contemporaries shared the confidence of the psalm writer who'd lived a thousand years earlier in King David's empire, declaring that just as Israel's king rules triumphant on earth, the Lord reigns supreme in heaven. Although some of Jesus's followers clung to the hope that someday such glory days would return, they, like the poet of the Job story, felt their faith shaken: If God really *were* in charge, how could his chosen messiah fail so miserably?

Reflecting on that story, I realized that despite his original ending, Mark had no intention of writing "bad news," as the philosopher Nietzsche later mocked him for doing. Now I began to see that Mark's decision to include Satan in the story does more than demonize people. Paradoxically, it also allows for hope, even when his raw narrative seems to offer none. For rather than give in to despair, Mark changes his vision of the supernatural world to show that evil is far more powerful than previously imagined. While refusing to give up hope that God reigns in heaven, Mark no longer sees his rule uncontested. Instead, he pictures Jesus living in a world in which evil forces have gained the upper hand and now virtually dominate—a scenario that resonated with many among his earliest audience, and with the experience of many people even now.

At the same time, Mark envisions Satan's power, however crushing, as temporary, soon to be eclipsed by divine miracle. Luke says that Jesus shared that vision and declared, "I saw Satan fall like lightning from heaven!" Thus the gospel writers can claim that instead of having failed, Jesus deliberately dared risk suffering, even death, to challenge the forces of evil, since he anticipated their eventual defeat. Perhaps because we all need hope, warranted or not, countless others who love these gospels have done the same. From the first century to now, followers of Jesus including the Lutheran pastor Dietrich Bonhoeffer, Roman Catholic archbishop Oscar Romero, Russian Orthodox Mary of Paris, and Baptist minister Martin Luther King Jr., each acutely aware of the power of hate, greed, and fear, nevertheless held on to what King called "a dream," a vision of justice and brotherhood, while taking action to realize it here and now. Every one of them knowingly risked death to do so, and was killed.

Now I could see that the story Mark tells would make little sense *without* Satan. Mark's vision of God's spirit contending against Satan enables him to tell a stark, unflinching account of Jesus's death, while picturing it as only a preliminary skirmish in a cosmic conflict now enveloping the universe. For as Mark sees it, the story he's telling doesn't end with death, or even at the grave site, where his own narrative ends so abruptly. Instead, he anticipates that just as Jesus prophesied, God's victory is coming soon—but *coming beyond the frame of his narrative, perhaps even beyond the frame of human history*. Seen this way, he writes not about failure, but about an unfinished victory.

Such stories stirred something in me, and I wondered, even though Mark and Heinz are dead, could there be something mysterious going on in the universe that we don't yet see? As I struggled to understand how these strange gospel stories became so deeply embedded in Western culture, and in my own imagination, I felt that their earliest writer, Mark, would not have dared announce "good news of Jesus of Nazareth, Messiah" had he not been convinced that some powerful divine mystery lay hidden in what he wrote. For even while telling how Jesus was tortured, mocked, and killed, Mark suggests that what looks like total defeat may end in hope. Throughout his story, Mark weaves in many hints to suggest that since God allowed his enemies to kill Jesus, his death must somehow have been "necessary": that it held secret meaning in a divine plan that Jesus alone understood.

He says, for example, that even on the night before Jesus died, he told his closest followers that the coming bloodshed would offer salvation "for many people," adding that even after his death, he looked forward to celebrating a triumph, when he would "drink new wine in the kingdom of God." And at the very moment when Jesus, on trial for his life, is sentenced to death, Mark pictures him warning the judge of his coming victory. Asked "Are you the Messiah, the Son of the Blessed One?" Jesus declares, *"Yes, I am; and you will see the Son of Man seated at the right hand of God, and coming with the clouds of heaven!"* Each of the later gospel writers echoes these themes of voluntary, meaningful suffering, so that instead of arousing rage and violent retaliation, the passion story often evokes wonder.

What people listening in the Colorado church that morning heard, I don't know. Even though I didn't share Mark's conviction, I could not help hoping that what happened might not wholly defeat us. And to my surprise, finishing my book on Satan felt like an exorcism. For those who find suffering inevitable—in other words, for any of us who can't dodge and pretend it's not there—acknowledging what actually happens is necessary, even if it takes decades, as it has for me. How, then, to go on living, without giving in to despair? I recalled lines from Wallace Stevens: "After the final *no*, there comes a *yes* / And on that *yes*, the future world depends. / *No* was the night. *Yes* is this present sun." Only when I began to awaken in the morning and see the sunlight, grateful for its warmth, could I dive into the secret gospels again. What was it I loved about them?

Besides our beloved teacher Krister Stendahl, who said that at first he thought these books were "just weird," others warned us not to read them—certainly not to love them. We'd seen how Bishop Irenaeus denounced them two thousand years ago as "recent writings," loved only by people too ignorant to discriminate between milk and poison, between genuine jewels and broken glass. But the *Gospel of Thomas*, which spoke to me from the day I first opened it, seemed to articulate what I often recall having seen, as if in a vision, on the day of Mark's funeral.

As Heinz and I walked out of the church on that day behind Mark's small wooden coffin, I had the sense that we were walking naked. We stood together in the vestibule as friends and colleagues came to embrace us. How could we possibly go on living? Did we even want to? At that moment, I desperately longed to escape from this life, seeking either our lost child or oblivion. It was then that I had seemed to see that vision of a huge net made of ropes, surrounding all of us, with open spaces through which we might be propelled into infinity, yet bound with knots that held us in this world. Later, someone told me of the Hindu image of the god Indra's net, embracing the world, often pictured blazing with jewels, or as a spiderweb hung with drops of dew. What I'd envisioned, instead, was a net of thick rope, with knots strong enough to anchor a ship in turbulent waters or tether an airplane in a hurricane. What drew me back to the *Gospel of Thomas* was a particular cluster of sayings that seemed to speak of what that vision meant—especially sayings that were previously unknown, strange, and compelling.

For unlike the *Gospel of Mark*, which pictures Jesus announcing that "the kingdom of God is coming soon," as a catastrophic event, the end of the world, the *Gospel of Thomas* suggests that he was speaking in metaphor:

> Jesus says: If those who lead you say to you, "The kingdom is in the sky," then the birds will get there first. If they say, "It is in the sea," then the fish will get there first. Rather, *the kingdom of God is within you, and outside of you. When you come to know yourselves* then . . . you will know that *you are the children of God.*

Here, with some irony, Jesus reveals that the kingdom of God is not an actual *place* in the sky—or anywhere else—or an *event* expected in human time. Instead, it's a state of being that we may enter when we come to know who we are, and come to know God as the source of our being.

In Thomas, then, the "good news" is not only about Jesus; it's also about every one of us. For while we ordinarily identify ourselves by specifying how we differ, in terms of gender, race, ethnicity, background, family name, this saying suggests that recognizing that we are "children of God" requires us to recognize how we are the same—members, so to speak, of the same family. These sayings suggest what later becomes a primary theme of Jewish mystical tradition: that the "image of God," divine light given in creation, is hidden deep within each one of us, linking our fragile, limited selves to their divine source. Although we're often unaware of that spiritual potential, the *Thomas* sayings urge us to keep on seeking until we find it: "Within a person of light, there is light. If illuminated, it lights up the whole world; if not, everything is dark." Emerging from a time of unbearable grief, I felt that such sayings offered a glimpse of what I'd sensed in that vision of the net. They helped dispel isolation and turn me from despair, suggesting that every one of us is woven into the mysterious fabric of the universe, and into connection with each other, with all being, and with God.

Once, when I spoke of this to another scholar, he objected. "Stop right there—now you're no longer writing history. What *use* is the *Gospel of Thomas* if you're simply reading your own experience into those cryptic sayings?" Like me, he'd first come to know these sayings through historical analysis, seeking to take into account all available evidence in order to understand them in their own linguistic, cultural, and historical context. But although such scholarship is necessary and valuable, it offers only limited understanding.

I chose to concentrate on these specific sources not only because they open up new historical perspectives, but also—and primarily—because I find them so compelling. However difficult it is to investigate a source we know only from a handful of Greek fragments and from a translation into Coptic, I love the challenge: while I work on these sayings, they work on me. My colleague's question also clarified that for many of us, the "use" of such poetic and mysterious words is *precisely* that we may discover our own experience in them. Many of us read them as we might read the Bible, the Koran, the sutras, or the poems that we love—not primarily for whatever they meant in the past, or for whoever wrote them down, but for what they might mean to us today.

What we're looking for may not be anything supernatural, as we usually understand what we call "spiritual." Instead, as one saying in *Thomas* suggests, we may find what we're seeking right where we are: "Jesus says: 'Recognize what is before your eyes, and the mysteries will be revealed to you.'" Like Emily Dickinson's poems, such sayings remain opaque as stone to anyone who has not experienced anything like what they describe; but those who have find that they open secret doors within us. And because they do, what each person finds there may be—*must* be—different. Each time we read them, the words may weave like music into a particular situation, evoking new insight. Some secret texts calm and still us, as when listening in meditation; others abound in metaphor, flights of imagination, soaring and diving.

During the years that followed, as I explored other texts from Nag Hammadi, I have found others, too, that strike me powerfully, and nurture hope. The poem called *Thunder, Com-*

plete Mind, for example, echoes how, for countless ages, people have heard thunder as a divine voice. But instead of envisioning the Lord Zeus speaking in thunder, as Greeks did, or Israel's God, as Jewish and Christian poets and prophets did, this poem personifies thunder—*bronte*, a feminine word in Greek—as a feminine power. Speaking in paradox, her voice confounds those who expect clarity, and frustrates those who need certainty. Here she declares that the divine presence, often unseen, shines everywhere, in all people, whether they live in palaces or garbage dumps, embracing all that we are. And instead of seeing the divine only in positive attributes like wisdom, holiness, and power, *Thunder* presses us to envision divine energy with our "complete mind," even in terms of negative experiences like foolishness, shame, and fear, as this short excerpt from the poem shows:

> I am the first and the last.
> I am the one who is honored, and the one scorned;
> I am the whore and the holy one . . .
> I am the incomprehensible silence,
> and . . . the voice of many sounds, the word in many
> forms;
> I am the utterance of my name . . .
> Do not cast anyone out, or turn anyone away . . .
> I am the one who remains, and the one who dissolves;
> I am she who exists in all fear,
> and strength in trembling.
> I am she who cries out . . .
> I am cast forth on the face of the earth . . .
> I am the sister of my husband,

and he is my offspring . . .

but he is the one who gave birth to me . . .

I am the incomprehensible silence

and the thought often remembered . . .

I am the one who has been hated everywhere,

and who has been loved everywhere.

I am the one they call Life, and you have called Death.

I am the one whose image is great in Egypt,

and the one who has no image among the barbarians . . .

I prepare the bread and my mind within;

I am the knowing of my name.

Whoever sang, chanted, or wrote *Thunder* wove Jewish, Egyptian, and Greek images into a single, complex pattern. One scholar, noting allusions to the *Genesis* creation story, suggested that the speaker is Eve, since some of these paradoxical lines allude to her Hebrew name, "Life," while Jewish and Christian sources accuse her of bringing death into the world ("I am the one they call Life, and you have called Death"). But rather than identifying the divine voice exclusively with Eve, this anonymous poet mentions her only as one of multiple forms through which this divine presence reveals herself. For as the next line suggests, the poet has adopted the form of a hymn to Isis, Egypt's divine protector, "she who is great in Egypt," praising her as another of thunder's countless manifestations. Noting that she "has no image among the barbarians," this poet, perhaps Greek or Egyptian, likely alludes to Jews, who startled their pagan neighbors by banishing feminine images from their visions of God. And it may have been women who especially delighted in *Thunder*, for even today, contemporary women artists including Leslie Marmon Silko, Toni Morrison, Julie Dash, and Kara Walker have loved this ancient poem and incorporated it into their own creative visions.

Other texts, some Christian, some not, speak of spiritual awakening in ways that "speak to my condition," as the Quakers say. The *Revelation of Zostrianos*, for example, speaks in the voice of a young man secretly planning to kill himself. After struggling for a long time to make sense of his life, and finding no answers to his most urgent questions, Zostrianos says that "I dared to act," walking alone into the desert "to deliver myself to the wild animals for a violent death." But as he steeled himself to do so, he says that suddenly he became aware of a luminous presence challenging him, saying, "Zostrianos, have you gone mad?" Zostrianos tells how, with huge relief, he turned to enter a cloud of light, which rescued him from despair and offered illumination. Finding new courage, he declares that "then I knew that the power in me was greater than the darkness, because it contained the whole light."

While Zostrianos recounts a sudden breakthrough, the source called *Allogenes* ("the stranger," in Greek) prescribes instead an intense, long-term practice of meditation and prayer. Here a spiritual teacher, Allogenes, perhaps mingling Jewish themes with elements of Buddhist tradition, tells his student Messos how he'd struggled to overcome his own fear, confusion, and mental turbulence, saying that a divine presence named Youel "gave me power" by teaching him to meditate, saying, "If you seek with everything you have, you shall come to know the good that is within you; and you will know yourself as one who comes from the God who truly exists."

Encouraged by Youel to withdraw temporarily when he is

afraid, Allogenes says he continued to practice for what seemed like an impossibly long time—a hundred years!—until his anxiety and mental turbulence began to subside. Then, he says, sometimes he experienced "a stillness of silence" in which "I knew my true self," until finally "I turned to myself and saw the light surrounding me, and the good within me, and I became divine." This doesn't mean that Allogenes thought he was God; rather, the Greek language that he speaks suggests that he felt he was experiencing his "true self" in continuity with "the unknown One." Yet even then, Allogenes speaks in language that mystics call the *via negativa*, the "negative way," acknowledging that the divine presence he occasionally glimpses is beyond human comprehension.

When we started working on these sources, many of us wondered why the monks who collected these texts included writings like this in their monastery library—writings that aren't even Christian. After coming to know these texts over time, I can only conclude that what mattered most to these monks wasn't dogma. They weren't judging the value of sacred writings by whether or not they conform to Christian doctrine. For the most part, the creeds by which later bishops defined who was Christian had not yet been invented. From the first to the mid-fourth century, before various creeds were increasingly formalized, many Christian monks were open to exploring other traditions along with their own, just as monastics today often include in their libraries writings that range from the works of Moses Maimonides to the Buddhist sutras; apparently they were less concerned with what to believe than with deepening their spiritual practice. Many people raised, even nominally, as I was, within Christian culture find Christianity's traditional exclusion of anything outside its boundaries too confining. And while finding truth for ourselves is difficult, often elusive, some of us can't avoid the challenge: instead, we dive in!

CHAPTER 8

Listening to Thunder

Sarah and David Pagels in Princeton, New Jersey, with Wolfgang,
thanks to Kent Greenawalt and Robert, Sasha, and Andrei.

On a brilliantly clear September morning, when the children were much older, I was walking to a breakfast meeting to welcome new students to the university when explosions in New York changed our world—two airplanes weirdly crashing into the World Trade towers, suddenly surreal scenes on television of the towers burning and crashing to the ground, countless people leaping out of the windows to die rather than burn alive; scenes of catastrophic confusion playing out like a horror movie, only shockingly real. Many scenes were unforgettable: George W. Bush vowing to lead a "crusade" against terror; Christian evangelicals denouncing homosexuals for bringing down God's wrath on this sinful nation; reporters hastily stumbling to account for Egyptian and Saudi engineers who'd come to American schools to learn to fly planes but not to land them, while planning this suicide mission.

What horrified many of us even more was that when the camps in Afghanistan where Osama bin Laden based his movement and trained his suicide bombers proved too difficult for American troops to find and subdue, the president and his allies rammed through Congress a plan to invade Iraq. Having traveled for decades to Israel, Egypt, and Africa, I was dumbfounded. And finally, since more than ten years had passed since Heinz's death, I was able to think about what this could mean for our nation. How could this war fail to turn Muslims throughout the world against America? Joining with many others, I protested; but although millions of us publicly opposed the war, our protests were banned from television news—suppressed—while nearly every member of Congress voted to support the president's planned invasion.

Even after Bush publicly censored his initial rallying cry for a crusade, he and his team sold the war as a battle of good against evil, invoking biblical language. "Shock and Awe," the popular name for the bombing of Baghdad, was meant to signal to believers that while the massive bombing might shock unbelievers, it would arouse awe among those who understood that American bombs were delivering God's righteous wrath. Like the president, many supporters of the war interpreted these events through the *Book of Revelation*'s prophecy that on the day of God's wrath, massive explosions and flashes of light would shatter Israel's ancient enemy, Babylon—today's Baghdad—as people on the ground writhed in agony, "cursing God" while dying, just as the Bible said they would. Later we learned that every day, George W. Bush, then president, received his intelligence briefing from Donald Rumsfeld's office with a quote from the Bible on the cover page to indicate that God endorsed the war.

As furious action raged all around us, religious visions and convictions fueled wartime fever, even—perhaps especially—when stated covertly, in culturally sanctioned code. Although I'd avoided the *Book of Revelation* since leaving that evangelical church as an adolescent, now I went back to read it again. This final book in the Bible is surely the strangest, consisting only of visions—dreams and nightmares, vivid with monsters, the Whore of Babylon, heaven and hell, and weird, unearthly creatures fighting wars that finally explode into the battle of Armageddon, when an angel from heaven, holding a key and a giant chain, seizes Satan, throws him into a bottomless pit, and locks and seals it for a thousand years. Then the dead are raised back to life from the sea and from Hades, to stand before a terrifying being seated on a great white throne who judges everyone who ever lived, allowing the righteous to enter the heavenly Jerusalem as it descends to earth, while casting evildoers into a lake of fire that burns forever.

How, I wondered, have these strange visions energized soldiers to fight in war for over a thousand years? The language of crusade seemed to come as naturally to a twentieth-century American president steeped in evangelical piety as it did to Christians in the seventh century, when Muslims attacked Constantinople, and in the eleventh century, when the Catholic king of France preached *Revelation*'s visions to fire up the armies he marched to the holy city of Jerusalem to fight the "infidels."

What astonished me even more is that warring antagonists *on both sides* of the same conflict often claim the same visions, seeing themselves as God's people and their opponents as Satan's; many still do. When Martin Luther's Reformation divided Christians throughout Europe, for example, Luther, who'd dismissed the *Book of Revelation* in 1523, saying "there's no Christ in it," endorsed it seven years later, after he realized how he could wield it as a weapon against the Catholic Church. So when he published his popular German translation of the Bible, eager to ensure that readers would interpret *Revelation* his way, Luther had the artist Lucas Cranach illustrate this book—and *only* this book—picturing the pope as the Whore of Babylon, seated on a seven-headed beast. Luther's first Catholic biographer struck back and published a hostile biography of Martin Luther prefaced with a caricature that pictures *him* as "the beast"—a seven-headed monster. Some years later, when war between Catholics and Protestants raged through

Europe, Protestants saw in *Revelation* a vision of their Protestant queen, Elizabeth I, as the heavenly woman "clothed with the sun," while Catholics pictured her as the Great Whore of Babylon.

Like countless others, Americans fighting wars later drew on that same resource. During the Civil War, a Mississippi artist pictured Lincoln being strangled by "the beast" that he labeled as the Union, while Julia Ward Howe's "Battle Hymn of the Republic" encouraged Union soldiers to fight their Confederate brethren with stirring words that she drew from *Revelation*. During World War II, Nazi propaganda minister Joseph Goebbels proclaimed that Adolf Hitler was about to fulfill *Revelation*'s prophecies and bring in the thousand-year reign of Christ—the third millennium (in German, *dritte Reich*)—after purifying the earth from massive human "pollution" that included unconverted Jews, the Roma people, homosexuals, and anyone who dared oppose Hitler. At the same time, during the freezing winter of 1941, when the French Catholic musician Olivier Messiaen, imprisoned in a Nazi prison camp, saw a rainbow in the sky, he recalled a scene from *Revelation* in which an angel haloed by a rainbow announces that "there shall be no more time." Messiaen then wrote his brilliant *Quartet for the End of Time*, which he and other prisoners performed for the prisoners and the guards.

And now, as if unable to wake from a nightmare, we watched wild visions we'd seen in fantasy films like *Star Wars* and *Lord of the Rings* catch fire again, fueling war. Since then, of course, some radical Muslims have adopted these same visions of God's victory over Satan and made them their own; even as the war party in the White House invoked biblical prophecies to justify invading Iraq, radical Muslims aroused jihadi to attack America, the "Great Satan."

I was amazed to see how powerfully John's *Book of Revelation* has engaged people in Western culture for two thousand years. How is it that these ancient biblical visions are still playing out in our politics? How can people claim to find contemporary events—different events, in each generation—prophesied in a book written two thousand years earlier? To find out, I went to the Princeton Theological Seminary Library, and was startled to find thousands of books about *Revelation* that packed an entire wall from floor to ceiling. What sense would it make to write one more? But as I worked my way through a huge pile of those books on the library's concrete floor, I could see that virtually all of them were written to interpret John's visions, or, at least, what each author thought his visions meant.

I was looking for something more down to earth. Who wrote this book, and why did he write as he did? What is it about his visions—or the way he tells them—that allows people to interpret them in wildly different ways? While engaged in that research, John's nightmare images invaded my dreams, and I kept wondering, *Who was John? What impelled him to write this?* And how can people still read his book today as if it were about their own time, not his?

This book is famously hard to understand, but it helps to know that it's wartime literature. John may have fled as a refugee from Jerusalem after 70 CE, when Roman armies finally defeated the Jewish revolutionaries, leaving the holy city in ruins. Hating the Romans, but wary of openly attacking Rome, while passionately longing for Israel's God to avenge his peoples' suffering, John did what Israel's classical prophets had done centuries earlier. He transposed the horrors of war into prophetic imagery, picturing Rome as Isaiah had pictured Israel's enemy Babylon, as a monster and whore. So John's *Book of Revelation* offers "imaginary gardens with real toads in them," as Marianne Moore said of poetry. But precisely because he *does* write in images so vivid and elemental that they appear in children's dreams, his readers have been able to plug them in, so to speak, to whatever conflict they confront. Countless people who have never read that book nevertheless have absorbed its pattern of interpreting conflict as nonnegotiable and war as the only possible response.

While offering some perspective on *Revelation*—and on the war fever swirling around me—these investigations alerted me to something I hadn't focused on before: that besides finding other gospels at Nag Hammadi, we'd also found many other books of revelation—not only *Thunder*, the *Revelation of Zostrianos*, and *Allogenes*, but also many Christian books of revelation. Surprised to see that John's *Book of Revelation* wasn't the *only* one, I then realized that, on the contrary, it was only one of an outpouring of "revelations" written around the end of the first century, not only by Christians but also by Jews, Greeks, Africans, Egyptians, and Syrians, and by prophets and worshippers of the many gods whose images filled cities throughout the Roman Empire.

But instead of prophesying about the end of time, the books of revelation found at Nag Hammadi often speak instead of spiritual breakthrough, as we've seen in the *Revelation of Zostrianos* and *Allogenes*. Another revelation widely read in antiquity, the *Secret Revelation of John*, tells how Jesus's disciple John, grieving after Jesus's death, suddenly felt the earth shake beneath his feet, saw brilliant light, and heard Jesus speaking to him from the light, saying, "John, John, why do you doubt, and why are you afraid? . . . I am the one who is with you always: I am the Father; I am the Mother; and I am the Son!" Then, John says, he was able to ask the risen Jesus the questions that weighed on his heart, and to receive consolation from the divine presence he now envisioned as the original trinity: heavenly Father, Son, and heavenly Mother, the Holy Spirit.

With so many people offering different "revelations," someone asked, how do we know which to trust? That question pushed me further: Why trust any? Why had I, or any of us, looked to "authorities" to validate our sense of what's true— whether what "the Bible says," as Billy Graham loved to claim, or what he or any other religious leaders say? Exploring these so-called heretical texts, I kept wondering what made church leaders regard them as so dangerous that they banded together to censor, bury, and burn them.

Like anyone engaged in spiritual search, those leaders knew that not everything that sounds like insight rings true. Religious fervor often veers so close to madness that some psychiatrists suspect that every religious emotion masks some kind of delusion. How can we tell truth from lies? What insights are genuine, and which are shallow, fearful, self-serving? The ancients, too, recognized these as the most difficult questions of all, since what they called "discernment of spirits"—discriminating between delusion and spiritual inspiration—requires wisdom. To simplify such questions, church leaders, seeing themselves as shepherds (*pastores*) worked to set clear boundaries—creeds and canon—to tell their "flocks" what to believe, what to read, and what *not* to read, while ordering them to look only to priests and bishops for guidance.

For when church leaders saw Christians in their congregations enthusiastic about sources like those found at Nag Hammadi—sources that don't prescribe what to believe, including some that aren't Jewish or Christian—some were intensely upset. Around 160 CE, Bishop Irenaeus, one of the most energetic leaders, insisted that his church was not only universal—"catholic"—but also possessed the only *absolute, unchanging truth* that could guarantee salvation. Some twenty-five years later, the African convert Tertullian, impatient with spiritual seekers, agreed with Irenaeus that such people were "heretics." Writing his famous prescription (*Rx*) to cure them from the potentially fatal disease of "heresy," he complained that "they're always quoting Jesus's saying, 'Seek, and you shall find,'" but "they never find anything, since they're looking where there's nothing to find." When such Christians challenged him, Tertullian ordered them to stop asking questions and accept what they're taught, famously warning that *"questions* are what make people heretics!"

For some of us, though, finding no easy answers doesn't mean that we can shut questions down. When, as an adolescent, I asked the questions that impelled me to leave that evangelical church ("Wasn't Jesus Jewish? Why do you imagine that a Jew who's not 'born again' is going to hell?"), I had to engage the challenge and keep asking. Later, as I explored the history of Christianity, another question continued to trouble me: Why do so many Christians, whether Catholic, Protestant, or Orthodox, insist that Jesus "had to die" before God could forgive human sin?

That question came up sharply the third morning after Mark died, when I walked through the carved wooden doors of the Church of the Heavenly Rest in New York, into the stone entrance hall to meet with clergy arranging a funeral for our son. Devastated, I was enormously grateful for the two friends who walked in with me. Elizabeth Diggs, our Lizzie, raised Episcopalian in Oklahoma, still loved some elements of that tradition, having discarded others, including Christianity's longtime hostility toward same-sex relationships; while Shulamith Gross, raised in an orthodox home in Israel, now a scientist, had left her family's traditions behind, except for Passover Seder.

As the heavy doors closed behind us, we heard someone reading the passion story; apparently he was practicing for the Good Friday service later that week. Walking up the long aisle leading toward the offices at the back of the church, I heard a familiar saying from the *Gospel of John*: "God so loved the world that he gave his only son" to die for our sins—and I stopped. Our only son had just died. At that moment, I felt that any god who did that—for *whatever* reason—would have to be crazy.

I wasn't taking the story literally, of course. To some extent, we can understand why Jesus's followers interpreted his death that way. Since worship in the Jerusalem temple required animal sacrifice, anyone desperately seeking for meaning might suggest that Jesus died as a human sacrifice, atoning for sin. When I was teaching at Princeton, years after high school, a friend from that time, the daughter of evangelical missionaries, called me after seeing the film *The Passion of the Christ* to tell me that she'd wept through Mel Gibson's graphic, endless scenes of torture, since they showed "how much God loves us."

Startled, I wondered, What kind of God lives in her imagination? An all-powerful god who, Christians say, "is love," and "loves the world," but who cannot, or will not, forgive human sin unless an innocent person—his own beloved son—is horribly tortured and slaughtered? Christians who preach that message also have to persuade potential converts that they are hopeless sinners, deservedly dangling over the fires of eternal torment, as revivalist preacher Jonathan Edwards, later president of Princeton University, pictured them in his famous sermon "Sinners in the Hands of an Angry God." Long before that, Saint Augustine shored up this dire fantasy by inventing "original sin," insisting that every human being, even a newborn baby, is born infected with mortal sin, which he pictured as a sexually transmitted *moral* disease. Both Roman Catholic and Protestant theologians, from Anselm through Martin Luther and Calvin, adopted Augustine's views, perhaps because they enabled each of them to claim that only his church could "save you." Evangelicals at Peninsula Bible Church in Palo Alto, where I'd gone as an adolescent, liked to repeat a perspective they often claim derives from the Hebrew Bible, "Without the shedding of blood there is no remission," almost singing the words, often earnest, sometimes smug, declaring that since "God so loved the world that he gave his only son to die for the sins of the world," you must "accept Jesus as your savior" or be damned.

Since this is the message that many proclaim, why not look elsewhere and abandon Christianity? I'd done that, and might never have returned for a deeper look had it not been for the secret gospels. Only much later did I realize that the formula basic to later Christian creeds ("Christ died for our sins") goes back to the apostle Paul—not, of course, to Jesus. What, then, did Paul preach as "good news"? Writing to converts in the Greek city of Corinth about twenty years after Jesus's death, he summed it up like this:

> *Christ died for our sins . . . he was buried, and raised* after three days, then appeared to Peter, then to the twelve, then to more than five hundred believers at once. . . . Last of all, he appeared to me.

Ever since leaving that evangelical church in Palo Alto, where Christians read Paul's letters as "God's word," I've disliked reading them. Although sometimes he writes powerfully, even poetically, often his tone is intensely domineering. His letters read as passionately written manifestos of an intense, impulsive, and brilliant missionary, bent on telling people what to believe and how to behave. Although he'd never met Jesus during his lifetime, Paul contemptuously dismissed those who had, angrily cursing even those who had known "the Lord" best—his closest disciple, Peter, and Jesus's own brother, James—when they disagreed with him about Jesus's message. But since Paul wrote his letters decades before others wrote gospels, and his recipients in Greece and Turkey copied them widely and sent them to potential converts all over the known world, they became primary documents of the early movement, his slogan "Christ crucified" often taken as the basic statement of the gospel.

Recently, though, in the *Gospel of Truth* found at Nag Hammadi, I discovered a different Paul—and a different message. Its anonymous author, most likely Valentinus, the Egyptian poet and visionary, who admires Paul, sees the apostle as teacher of secret wisdom whose vision of grace includes everyone. Having carefully read the letters of Paul now in the New Testament, this author writes what he calls "the true gospel" to answer a question that Paul leaves dangling in his famous first letter to the Corinthians.

Paul had opened that letter saying that when he first arrived in Corinth, he was upset and dismayed to find believers arguing about what the basic message—the "good news"—actually was. Disagreeing, they'd split into factions, each following a different teacher, some saying, "I belong to Peter['s group]," others saying, "I belong to Paul's," some to groups that others led. Determined to stop controversy and create one unified group based on what he called "*my* gospel," Paul scolded believers in Corinth, telling them that since "you were babies in Christ, I could only feed you milk—baby food."

Once he realized this, he says, "I didn't come to you, brothers, proclaiming the mystery of God, in exalted speech or wisdom," the "meat" that he would have given to people who were spiritually mature. Instead, he says, "I decided among you" to preach only the simplest, most basic version of the gospel, nothing but "Jesus Christ crucified"—hardly more than a slogan, foolish as he knew it would sound to educated people. For Paul says that he realized even "the foolishness of my message," that is, "the message about the cross," could suffice "to save those who believe."

But writing to the Corinthians, Paul hastens to add that he's not preaching this simpleminded message because it's all that he knows. On the contrary, he says, he *does* teach secret wisdom to those who are spiritually mature:

> We *do* teach wisdom among people who are mature—not
> the wisdom of this world, nor of the rulers of this age.
> Rather, *we speak the wisdom of God hidden in mystery,*
> which God foreordained before the ages for our glory—
> which none of the rulers of this age knew—for, had they
> known it, they would not have crucified the Lord of glory.

I was intrigued to see that here, in his own words, Paul hints
at a different version of the gospel—not that God "sent his own
son to die" as a human sacrifice, but that ignorant and violent
people, or the spiritual powers that energized them, had killed
Jesus. Yet then he goes on to say that despite their malice, this
awful event concealed a mystery. Surely he intended his mysterious words to raise intense curiosity: What, or who, *is* that primordial "wisdom of God, hidden in mystery"—secret wisdom,
unknown even to the most powerful people in the world? And
why does Paul refuse to tell them?

Instead of answering, Paul leaves these questions dangling
and remains provocative, tempting and teasing his audience by
adding that no human being could possibly imagine "what God
has prepared for those who love him." Only those whom God's
spirit teaches directly, as Paul claims the spirit taught him, could
know what he calls "the deep things of God." But, he says, he's
withholding that secret wisdom from them, since he can only
tell it to "the mature"—and, he says, "You're not that, so I'm giving you only the simplest message: 'Christ crucified.' "

What, then, *is* the true gospel? Fascinated, I realized that
the anonymous author of the *Gospel of Truth* writes to answer
that question, and to reveal that secret wisdom—or, at least, his
version of it. He begins with the words *"The true gospel is joy,* to

those who receive from the Father the grace of knowing him!" Plunging into that mystery, he says that the *true* gospel, unlike the simple message, doesn't begin in human history. Instead, it begins *before* this world was created.

What happened, then, not just "in the beginning," but *before* the beginning, in primordial time—and how would we know? To answer this question, the *Gospel of Truth* offers a poetic myth. For around the time this author was writing, some devout Jews, and some non-Jews as well, loved to speculate on questions about what God was doing before he created the world. Often they looked for hidden meaning in poetic passages of the Hebrew Bible, like that opening line from *Genesis*, which tells how "a wind (or spirit, *ruah*) from God moved over chaotic deep waters." What *was* there, then? Others claimed to find hints of what happened in a famous poem in the biblical *Book of Proverbs*, in which divine wisdom (*hohkmah*), identified with God's spirit (*ruah*), tells how she worked with God to create the world. Since both "spirit" and "wisdom" are feminine terms in Hebrew, she speaks as the Lord's feminine companion, or perhaps as his beloved daughter, who participated with him in creating the world, when first she swept over the deep ocean waters:

> When he marked out the foundations of the earth, I was there beside him, like a little child, delighting him daily, always rejoicing before him, and rejoicing in his world full of people, delighting in the human race.

Whoever wrote the poem called *Thunder, Complete Mind* apparently drew on that opening line of *Genesis*, as well as on the poem in *Proverbs*, as did another anonymous writer whose poem was found at Nag Hammadi, who also gave a feminine voice to the primordial, life-giving energy that brings forth all things:

> I am the thought that lives in the light.
> I live in everyone, and I delve into them all . . .
> I move in every creature. . . .
> I am the invisible one in all beings . . .
> I am a voice speaking softly . . .
> I am the real voice . . . the voice from the invisible
>   thought . . .
> It is a mystery . . . I cry out in everyone . . .
> I hid myself in everyone, and revealed myself within
>   them, and every mind seeking me longs for me . . .
> I am she who gradually brought forth everything . . .
> I am the image of the invisible spirit . . .
> The mother, the light . . . the virgin . . . the womb, and the
>   voice . . .
> I put breath within all beings.

Some, then, drew on passages they found in the Bible, and on the famous creation myth that Plato tells in his dialogue *Timaeus*, to spin stories about what happened in primordial time. But certain rabbis, wary of such speculations, tried to shut them down, fiercely forbidding anyone to speak about "what happened before, or beyond, or above" the world's creation. The Christian bishop Irenaeus vehemently agreed with such rabbis, insisting, as they did, that human beings were never meant to know such mysteries, much less to probe into them.

But prohibitions have never stopped people from speculating. When Paul and his followers wanted to claim that *Jesus* existed even before the world was created, they drew on Jewish poems and myths about divine wisdom—ignoring the gender difference—to say that *Jesus Christ* was himself that "hidden mystery" who worked with God to create the world. So when the author of the *Gospel of Truth* sets out to reveal Paul's secret teaching, he begins by asking, What happened *before* the beginning of time?

In answer, he offers a primordial drama of creation, telling how, when "all beings" began to search for the One from whom they came forth, they couldn't find him. Feeling abandoned, not knowing where they came from, they suffered anguish and terror, like children wandering in the dark, searching in vain for their lost parents. As this gospel tells it, what separates all beings, including ourselves, from God is not *sin*. Instead, what frustrates our longing to know our source is its transcendence, and our own limited capacity for understanding. Yet when these beings—or when we—realize that we can't find our way home, don't know where we came from, or how we got here, we feel utterly lost. Overwhelmed by grief and fear, we may rush into paths that lead nowhere, more lost than ever, imagining that there's nothing beyond the confusion we see in the world around us.

At this point, the *Gospel of Truth* turns toward a drama of cosmic redemption. When the Father sees his children terrified and suffering, ensnared by negative energies, he sends his Son, "the hidden mystery, Jesus the Christ," to show them a path and bring them back "into the Father, into the Mother, Jesus of the infinite sweetness." And although, as Paul says in *1 Corinthians*, ignorant and violent "rulers of this world" tortured and crucified Jesus, the Father overturned their conspiracy, transforming even their hideous crime into a means of grace.

To show this, the *Gospel of Truth* reframes the vision of the cross from an instrument of torture into a *new* tree of knowledge. Here Jesus's battered body, "nailed to a tree," is seen as fruit on a tree of "knowing the Father," which unlike that tree in Paradise, doesn't bring death, but life, to those who eat from it. Thus the author suggests that those who participate in the Eucharist, eating the bread and drinking the wine that, symbolically speaking, are Jesus's flesh and blood, "discover him in themselves" while he "discovers themselves in him."

After years of contending with familiar Jewish and Christian sources, I found here a vision that goes beyond what Paul calls "the message of the cross." Instead of seeing suffering as punishment, this gospel suggests that, seen through the eyes of wisdom, suffering can show how we're connected with each other, and with God; what Paul's letter to the Colossians calls "the mystery of Christ in you, the hope of glory." No wonder, then, that Christians called their sacred meal a mystery (*mysterion*), a Greek term later translated as "sacrament" (from Latin *sacramentum*).

The *Gospel of Truth* then offers, in poetic language, other transformed images of the cross. The author clearly knows that Jesus's early followers often pictured the cross as a post for publishing official announcements. Matthew's gospel, giving a literal interpretation, says that Pilate ordered his soldiers to post his death sentence on the cross, worded to mock his Jewish subjects: "Jesus of Nazareth, King of the Jews." Sometime later, Paul, or whoever wrote the New Testament letter to the Colossians in his name, suggested instead that what was written on the cross wasn't *Pilate's sentence against Jesus*, but rather *God's "sentence of condemnation against us"*—the death sentence we deserved for our sins.

But the author of the *Gospel of Truth* rejects the picture of God that both images imply—God as a harsh, divine judge who sent Jesus into the world "to die for our sins." Instead, he suggests, the loving and compassionate Father sent Jesus to find those who were lost, and to bring them back home. So rather than see the writing on the cross as *any* death sentence—whether Pilate's or God's—this author suggests instead that Jesus published there "the living book of the living," a book "written in our heart" that teaches us who we really are, since it includes the names of everyone who belongs to God's family.

Now this author breaks into praise, marveling that "love made a body" for Jesus as he voluntarily descended into this world, even knowing that he'd have to suffer and die in order to "publish that book": "O such great teaching! He draws himself down to death, although eternal life clothes him ... entering into the empty spaces of terror ... stripping himself of the perishable to put on imperishability." This vision suggests that suffering and death are simply the necessary cost of entering into human life, motivated by love.

The *Gospel of Truth*, then, is all about relationships—how, when we come to know ourselves, simultaneously we come to know God. Implicit in this relationship is the paradox of *gnosis*— not intellectual knowledge, but knowledge of the heart. What first we must come to know is that we cannot fully know God, since that Source far transcends our understanding. But what we can know is that we're intimately connected with that divine Source, since "in him we live and move and have our being."

As I imagine it, around the time this gospel was written, someone told this story to men and women fasting and staying awake all night in darkness, as they waited to be baptized into Christ's family on Easter morning, telling them, "This is your story, and mine." For as we've seen, when the storyteller talks about "all beings," he's also talking about *us*. Although Bishop Irenaeus ridicules "heretics" for telling such stories in myth, this is myth as Plato told it: imagination revealing the deeper truths of human experience. So, the speaker concludes, *"If, indeed, these things have happened to each one of us,"* then we can see that this mythical story has real consequences.

Those who lack the sense of connection with others, and with the source of all being, live, he says, as if in a nightmare:

> As if we were asleep, deep in disturbing dreams; either running in terror, or as if we are striking out, or receiving blows, or falling from high places, or as if someone were murdering them, or they themselves are filling their neighbors, for they have been stained with their blood.

Those who recognize this story as their own, as I do, may realize how this "nightmare parable" coincides with experience. We all know that people who feel isolated, overwhelmed by terror and anger, can turn their own nightmares into horrific reality, from the inner cities of our nation to war-ravaged cities throughout the world.

On the other hand, when we recognize how connected we are with one another and with "all beings," this author says, we may "say from the heart that you are the perfect day;

in you dwells the light that does not fail." And recognizing this, in turn, impels us to act in ways that acknowledge those connections:

> Speak the truth with those who search for it . . . support those who have stumbled, and extend your hands to those who are ill. Feed those who are hungry; give rest to the weary . . . strengthen those who wish to rise; and awaken those who are asleep.

Is this really Paul's secret teaching? We can't know for sure. As we've seen, some scholars agree that the renowned Egyptian teacher Valentinus wrote this gospel, since its language resonates with a famous poem that he wrote, and with the few fragments of his teaching that survive. Did the author receive Paul's secret teaching orally, handed down in succession from a disciple named Theudas, who received it from Paul? Maybe so, since that's what Valentinian tradition claims; alternatively, its author may have drawn on Paul's letters to write it himself. But whoever wrote it wasn't trying to impress the reader, since he doesn't consider his own name worth mentioning, and doesn't specifically claim that Paul wrote it. Instead, the story he tells speaks for itself—or doesn't—depending on who's reading it.

I've come to love this poetic and moving story for the way it reframes the gospel narrative. Instead of seeing suffering as punishment, or somehow as "good for you," this author sees it rather as Buddhists do, as an essential element of human existence, yet one that may have the potential to break us open out of who we are. My own experience of the "nightmare"—the agony of feeling isolated, vulnerable, and terrified—has shown that only awareness of that sense of interconnection restores equanimity, even joy.

But while this myth "speaks to my condition," many other sources do as well, and it may not speak to yours. Through teaching and talking with friends, I've come to see how differently various people interpret their lives, depending on temperament and situation, as psychologist William James shows in his classic book *The Varieties of Religious Experience*. James wrote *Varieties* after he recovered from a crippling depression by clinging to certain religious slogans, even though he says that he didn't actually believe them. Still, the experience was so compelling that it led him to investigate case studies of conversion, and to challenge Freud's view that religion is nothing but illusion.

James defines religion instead as a person's "total reaction upon life." Drawing on poems, philosophy, accounts of conversion, reports of healing, and claims of mystical union, he notes, for example, how Walt Whitman's ebullient poetry may appeal particularly to optimists, while more cerebral, emotionally controlled people may prefer Marcus Aurelius's Stoic philosophy. Of course, these need not be separate categories; both might speak to any of us in different ways. James goes on to note that people experiencing intense internal conflict often identify with what the apostle Paul and Saint Augustine say of their own emotional turmoil in accounts that, even today, people ranging from Catholics and evangelical Christians to members of Alcoholics Anonymous take as models for conversion. And since James was acutely aware that religious experience often looks like psychosis, he was especially intrigued by what religious radicals, saints, and mystics report of visions, voices, and extreme mood shifts, such as Count Leo Tolstoy's account of recovery from suicidal depression, which lent James perspective on his own recovery.

Some of the books found at Nag Hammadi include a similar scattershot range of sources, often bound into the same volumes. Like William James, the second-century Christian author of the *Gospel of Philip* observes that people of different temperaments, situations, and levels of insight need different kinds of spiritual "food." And just as James turns from Whitman's poems to Stoic philosophy, whoever compiled Nag Hammadi's sixth book placed the poem called *Thunder* next to a passage from Plato's *Republic*. Yet while William James focuses primarily on Christian sources, and tends to ignore collective and ritual aspects of religious experience, some of these ancient scribes embraced a far wider cultural range, apparently less concerned, as we've seen, with *belief* than with *approaches to spiritual practice*. For then, as now, city people and travelers lived in a cosmopolitan world, in which the second-century Greek-speaking Christian in Rome named Hippolytus knew of "naked Hindus by the Ganges," whom he called "heretics." At the same time, Indian sculptors were producing images of the Buddha influenced by the conventions of Greek sculptors; and the author of *Allogenes*, perhaps Jewish, may have incorporated Buddhist practice into his "revelation." And although I think it's extremely unlikely that Jesus spent his "lost years" in India, as some people like to speculate, Syrian Christian tradition suggests that the apostle Thomas brought Jesus's teachings to India, where Hindu or Buddhist teaching may have influenced some sayings now found in the *Gospel of Thomas*.

Book VI from Nag Hammadi, for example, mixes a wide range of perspectives, starting with a story of how the twelve apostles, fearful and discouraged after Jesus's death, meet a doctor who calls himself a "physician of souls"—the literal translation of the word "psychiatrist"—who turns out to be Jesus. Suddenly revealing himself, Jesus offers them a box of ointments and a medicine pouch, saying, "first heal [peoples'] bodies," and then "heal the heart." Six more sacred texts follow this story—are these meant to be their "medicines"? If so, this ancient scribe offers prescriptions that range from *Thunder*, which celebrates the divine presence shining through the world, to Plato's *Republic* and the *Discourse on the Eighth and the Ninth*, a ritual text in which a spiritual "father" teaches a young, impatient disciple to chant and pray, "singing in silence," so that he may attain ecstatic union with the Greek god Hermes. This volume closes with another short text on the "mystery of sexual intercourse" and a prayer, both dedicated to Asclepius, Greek god of healing. Other books in this collection, as we've seen, include Zostrianos's story of his surprise encounter with the divine presence that rescued him from despair, and *Allogenes*, which prescribes what another person might find healing: an intense, disciplined practice of meditation. So I like to imagine that whoever bound these diverse texts together may have had a perspective something like that of William James—that when Jesus, or anyone else, acts as "physician of souls," the "medicine chest" might include a variety of treatments, depending on each patient's need and response.

What these sources do show is that many people in antiquity spent enormous time and energy searching for ways to "heal the heart," as countless people are doing today, expanding an enormously increased range of chemical medications, therapeutic techniques, exercises, and support groups, as well as practices of meditation and yoga. And while my own plunge into the history of religion began after that first explosive experience with evangelical Christianity, what happened during our son's illness and death, followed so soon afterward by my husband's death, compelled me to search for healing beyond anything I'd ever imagined.

What's found in the secret gospels, and throughout the process of exploring the history of religion, offers resources we're now beginning to appreciate. What also helped me was Heinz's insight and imagination, shaped by scientific inquiry, which often extends beyond personal suffering. Once, as noted before, when he saw me in anguish after we received our child's crushing diagnosis, he said something I often recall: *"Everyone's life has something like this in it."* Angry, I snapped back; "No, not *this*—not a child with a terminal illness!" "No," he said, "not *this*, but something like this." Much later, I came to realize how much truth there is in what he said. Even now, writing about what's so deeply personal, I'm aware that anything I say can speak to you only as it resonates through what you have experienced yourself; yet even within those limits, we may experience mutual recognition.

A few years ago, I was astonished to receive a letter from Drew Faust, then president of Harvard, inviting me to accept an honorary degree from my graduate school. When I opened that letter, thoughts tumbled in fast: first, "How amazing, when she has so many people to choose from—" then immediately, "But Heinz won't be there—" as he was when I received my graduate degree. How could I go back there without him? But then Sarah, now twenty-six and married, agreed to come with her husband and their adorable two-year-old twins, Thomas and Rebekah;

and David, twenty-five, would fly from Utah with his girlfriend to join us, so I gladly accepted.

On the morning of the ceremony, converging from Utah, Colorado, and New Jersey at the Boston hotel the university had booked for us, we took Thomas and Rebekah to the public gardens, where they delighted in seeing the ducks and swans, and we rode on the merry-go-round. Then we headed for Cambridge, since university officials had said that thirty-two thousand people would pack into Harvard Yard for the day's celebration. The June sun was already hot as families, children, grandparents, and friends of the graduates crowded the sidewalks, dressed to celebrate, warding off the heat with fans and sunglasses as we pressed toward the wrought-iron university gates.

Because the names of those receiving honorary degrees are kept secret until that morning, only when nine of us gathered by one of the gates did we meet some of the others: José Antonio Abreu, musician and activist from Venezuela; Donald Hopkins, the distinguished African American physician; Tom Menino, the beloved mayor of Boston, and, most recognizable of all, Oprah Winfrey, excited and joyful, nearly dancing as she led our procession into the Yard. Seeing her, many graduates gasped with surprise, cheering and shouting, begging her to stop for them, which she often did, laughing and hugging them as they took photos. Trumpets blazed and drummers beat time as we joined an enormous parade, thousands of graduates dressed in black robes, those from the graduate schools robed in bright crimson, and the faculty, like a flock of iridescent birds, robed in brilliant blue, orange, red, gold, black, and purple, led by marshals in formal dress and top hats through the dense crowd of celebrators.

In spite of all the pomp and formality, it felt like a huge and glorious party.

When we reached the platform, people meeting, talking, laughing, greeting, I recalled how, decades before, I'd been among that dense crowd of graduates. Marveling at the celebration going on all around us, and enjoying the entire spectacle, I loved hearing the stories of others sitting near: how José Abreu had founded the project he called El Sistema, which enables impoverished inner-city children throughout the world to join youth orchestras and play music together; how Donald Hopkins had helped eradicate smallpox throughout the world. Tom Menino had just arrived from a hospital bed, determined to join the celebration, while only months before, he'd calmed a city horrified by violence, after bombs killed and maimed people on the morning of the Boston Marathon; and Oprah Winfrey spoke with candor, humility, and humor, encouraging the graduates to persist, as she has, through difficulty and failure.

Sitting there, feeling waves of revelry and emotion pass through that huge crowd, I was suddenly stopped: *Where are they, those who aren't here, now lost to us?* But as the music blared, and the prayers, introductions, and speeches echoed over the microphones, I saw Sarah and David sitting among the families. Suddenly a storm of tears and gratitude broke through me, as I felt, unexpectedly, that I was also graduating, along with those thousands of others. How, I wondered, had I somehow managed to pass the *real* tests—the tests I never could have imagined surviving, those unimaginable losses? Yet the children left for me to raise were both here, alive and well, and so am I: How is that possible?

I don't know how to answer those questions. What I *do* know is that for moments, during that noisy and joyful ceremony, the pomp and privilege of that scene receded, and the invisible bonds connecting everyone there, and connecting all of us with countless others and with our world and whatever is beyond it, felt stronger than ever, echoing the words of an ancient Jewish prayer: "Blessed art Thou, Lord God of the Universe, that you have brought us alive to see this day." However it happens, sometimes hearts *do* heal, through what I can only call grace.

Acknowledgments

This is a book I never thought I could write, as noted at the start—and surely could not have written without the encouragement and help that family members, friends, and colleagues have generously given. And since asking friends to read a manuscript, or some part of it, is asking an enormous favor, I'm especially grateful to those who have been willing to do that, and who have offered comments, corrections, and suggestions that have much improved the manuscript throughout seven to eight years of writing. Each of them is well aware of the personal experiences involved, as well as elements of the history of religion woven into them: Sandie Berman, Timothy Brown, Elizabeth Diggs, Phoebe Graubard, Linda Hess, Victoria Juedt, Lyn Lear, Catherine Mauger, Emily McCully, Diane Morris, Susan Morrow, John Pollock, Arnold Rampersad, Judith Schramm, Tracy K. Smith, Idamae Trenner, Marvina White, Michael Wood.

I am grateful to longtime friends John Brockman and Katinka Matson, who encouraged me to write when we first began discussing this book; and to Dan Halpern, president and publisher of Ecco, HarperCollins, whose enthusiasm and expertise helped me as I wrote, and who guided me to my wonderful editor, Denise Oswald. Many thanks to Emma Janaskie and Ashley Garland for taking this book through the process of production, and carefully taking care of so many details; and to my colleagues, Dr. Lance Jenott and Dr. George Rambow, each of whom offered expert assistance in research, while participating in preparing the manuscript and endnotes.

I owe special thanks to Jason Epstein, who, years ago, as editorial director of Random House, took a chance on *The Gnostic Gospels*, and taught me how to write, turning language learned in graduate school, which sounded like a text badly translated from German, into something readable. Ever since, including with this present book, he has generously offered the indispensable expert advice for which he's renowned. I cannot thank him enough.

I'm especially grateful to those who helped make possible the year's leave on sabbatical from Princeton University that allowed me to finish writing. First of all, thanks to Caroline Winterer, director of the Humanities Center at Stanford University; and Andrea Davies, associate director, who invited me to visit the Humanities Center in the spring of 2017, as the Marta Sutton Weeks Distinguished Visitor, to give a lecture on Satan—which turned out to be a popular topic!—and to enjoy the company of colleagues and friends at Stanford. Michael Wood, Leora Batnitsky, and Lorraine Furhmann graciously—and ingeniously—worked out appropriate arrangements with Princeton University. Many thanks, too, to those whose presence made the visit to Stanford so enjoyable—to Tanya Luhrmann and Richard Saller, for their collegiality, scholarship, and marvelous hospitality; to Robert and Mary Ellin Gregg, Kathryn Gin, Kirsti and Mychal Copeland, Jane Shaw, and Linda Hess, my former Stanford roommate; and to Marvina White and Arnold Rampersad, both of whom also generously helped with the writing.

During the years of the writing, I've been acutely aware of how fortunate I am to be teaching at Princeton University, with colleagues whose great capacity for collegiality and friendship I deeply appreciate, from those in our subfield—Martha Himmelfarb, Anne Marie Luijendijk, Moulie Vidas, and Laura Quick—as well as many others, including Leora Batnitsky, Wallace Best, Judith Weisenfeld, and Jonathan Gold. Thanks to Jeffrey Guest, for countless "saves" from disastrous computer meltdowns; and to Mary Kay Bodnar, Kerry Smith, and Lorraine Furhmann, for everything they do every day for all of us, with such a generous spirit. Special thanks to Richard Trenner, for the time and artistry he took to help find the right jacket photograph; and to Barbara Conviser, friend and artist, who took the photograph of me now on the jacket, and generously gave permission for me to use it.

I owe special thanks, too, to my dear friend the late James Cone, who read all the drafts, suggested changes that much improved some chapters, and talked with me about this book and his, as this book emerged simultaneously with his most recent book *Said I Wasn't Going to Tell Nobody*. And I'm grateful to Serene Jones, president of Union Theological Seminary, for her great generosity to him, and also for her hospitality; and to Professor Kelly Brown, whose clear, calm, incisive, and generous presence helped steady all of us, including his sons, Charles and Michael; and his daughter-in-law, Janie; and his daughters, Robyn and Krystal, as we walked together, so far as possible, through the great loss of their remarkable and loving father.

Finally, I am grateful to those whose presence and encouragement, in ways known to each of them, have helped see me through these years, and mention in particular Elizabeth Diggs and Emily McCully, Catherine Mauger, Emily Mann and Gary Mailman; Jane Shapiro, Sandie Berman, Jeanne Carter, Idamae Trenner, Barbara Conviser; Judith Schramm, John Pollock, David Stout, Michael and Elena Wood, and Marvina White; to fellow members of "Margot's group," for the joy of our sustained friendship and shared meditation; and to Paul and Christina Jeanes, and their wonderful family, including Sophie, John Paul, Luke, Leslie, and Maria.

I owe most personal thanks to Kent Greenawalt for our ongoing close relationship, and to Andrei, Sasha, and Robert Greenawalt; to my daughter, Sarah, and her children, and her partner, Mark Toussaint; to my son David, and his extended family, including Len and Danielle Strickman; and to April, Jake, and Grace Harris.

Notes

CHAPTER 1: WHY RELIGION?

23 According to saying 70: *Gospel of Thomas* (NHC II,2), saying 70.

26 The anonymous author: *Gospel of Truth* (NHC I,3), 18:29–31.

29 To stanch the flow: Irenaeus, *Against Heresies*, III.11.9.

29 They even put forth: Ibid., III.15.2, and *Preface*.

29 Mark's gospel says: *Mark* 4:10–12.

30 Even today, you can find: See, for example, the commentary by conservative scholar Simon Gathercole, *The Gospel of Thomas: Introduction and Commentary* (Leiden, The Netherlands: Brill Academic Publishing, 2014).

31 Nearly two hundred: Athanasius, *Pascal Letter*, 39.

33 What I love: *Gospel of Thomas* (NHC II,2), saying 25. In these and other citations from the *Gospel of Thomas*, the translation is the one that Marvin Meyer and I did together, published in *Beyond Belief: The Secret Gospel of Thomas* (New York: Random House, 2004).

33 "Knock upon yourself": *The Teachings of Silvanus* (NHC VII,4), 106:30–35.

33 While urging us: *Gospel of Thomas* (NHC II, 2), saying 2.

33 And when asking: Ibid., saying 5.

CHAPTER 2: LOVE AND WORK

42 Terrified, John says: *The Apocryphon ("Secret Revelation") of John* (NHC II,1), 2:9–14.

43 Furthermore, nearly two thousand: Irenaeus, *Against Heresies*, I.21.3.

44 Becoming arrogant in spirit: Ibid., I.30.6. Note how sources found at Nag Hammadi confirm his account; see, for example, *The Hypostasis of the Archons* (a.k.a. *The Reality of the Rulers*) (NHC II,4), 94:19–26, and *On the Origin of the World* (NHC II,5), 103:3–18. For a fuller discussion, see Elaine Pagels, *The Gnostic Gospels* (New York: Random House, 1979), chapter 3: "God the Father, God the Mother."

44 Two thousand women: *The Apocryphon of John* (NHC II,1) 20:9–21:1.

44 Certain rabbis, playing: *The Midrash Rabbah, Genesis* XX.10.

44 So, this author: *Testimony of Truth* (NHC IX,3), 47:28–48:1.

45 Some versions of this story: *Genesis* 3:16.

45 These heretical women: Tertullian, *Prescription Against Heretics*, in: *The Ante-Nicene Christian Library: Translations of the Writings of the Fathers down to A. D. 325*, Volume 3, eds. A. Roberts and J. Donaldson (Edinburgh: T&T Clark, 1866–72).

46 Now that the people: Professor Raymond Brown, a prominent scholar of New Testament, called them that in his negative review of my book *The Gnostic Gospels* on the front page of the *New York Times Book Review*, "The Christians Who Lost Out" (January 20, 1980).

51 There, too, we met: Francis Deng, *Dinka Folktales: African Stories from the Sudan* (New York: Holmes & Meier, 1984).

53 The first story: *Genesis* 1:28.

55 I do not allow: *1 Timothy* 2:12–1.

55 "You are the devil's": Tertullian, *On Women's Clothes*, 1.12, in: *The Ante-Nicene Christian Library: Translations of the Writings of the Fathers down to A. D. 325*, Volume 4, eds. A. Roberts and J. Donaldson (Edinburgh: T&T Clark, 1866–72).

56 Are we to believe: *Genesis* 3:8.

56 The anonymous author: *Testimony of Truth* (NHC IX,3), 49:8.

56 Others read the story: *The Apocryphon of John*; for discussion, see Elaine Pagels, *Adam, Eve, and the Serpent: Sex and Politics in Early Christianity* (New York: Random House, 1988), 65–68.

CHAPTER 4: GOING ON

95 Only decades later: Clifford Geertz, "Religion as a Cultural System," in: *The Interpretation of Cultures: Selected Essays* (Fontana Press, 1993), 87–125.

101 Biblical stories often suggest: *2 Kings* 2:23–25.

103 When popularizing the teaching: Lucretius, *De Rerum Natura (On the Nature of the Universe)*, V.110–112.

103 Like Lucretius, Freud: See, for example, Sigmund Freud, *The Future of an Illusion* (New York: W. W. Norton & Company, 1989).

CHAPTER 6: LIFE AFTER DEATH

141 "Although grief therapists": Renato Rosaldo, "Grief and a Headhunter's Rage," in *Culture and Truth: The Remaking of Social Analysis* (Boston: Beacon Press, 1989), 10.

142 Only this, his informants: Ibid., 11.

142 Finding her body: Ibid., 9.

142 At the time he wrote: Ibid., 11.

143 When Cain's anger boils: *Genesis* 4:6–7.

144 The Bible's Exodus stories: *Exodus* 15:7.

144 Summoning the Levites: Ibid., 15:27.

144 Then he announces: Ibid., 32:7–29.

144 But he ends: *2 Samuel* 24:1–16.

145 But as the angel: *1 Chronicles* 21:1–14.

149 While mourning his dead: *Job* 1:1–22.

149 The *Book of Job* ends: Ibid., 42:7b–17.

149 But as the third: Ibid., 3:1–25.

149 But when he fails: Ibid., 16:7–9; 9:24.

150 Now Job confronts: Ibid., 38:1–7; 40:15–41:22.

153 We need to stop: Victor Frankl, *Man's Search for Meaning*, (Boston: Beacon Press, 2006), 77.

156 Reading a book: Jeffrey Burton Russell, *The Devil: Perceptions of Evil from Antiquity to Primitive Christianity* (Ithaca, NY: Cornell University Press, 1970), 3.

157 Anyone entering this: IQS, *Serekh ha-Yadah* (Community Rule), 1.

160 As Mark tells it: *Mark* 15:1–15.

160 Everything we know: For details and discussion, see Elaine Pagels, *The Origin of Satan* (New York: Random House, 1995), 10, 29–33.

160 Mark's successors added: *Matthew* 27:25.

160 And John's gospel: *John* 8:44.

160 "Christian prejudices against": T. Barnes, *Constantine and Eusebius* (Cambridge, MA: Harvard University Press, 1981), 252: "Constantine translated Christian prejudice against the Jews into legal disabilities."

161 Throughout two thousand: For discussion, see Jessica Stern, *Terror in the Name of God: Why Religious Militants Kill* (New York: Ecco, 2004).

CHAPTER 7: WRESTLING WITH THE DEVIL

167 The biblical story: *Genesis* 19:4.

167 Another Bible story: *2 Samuel* 11:26–12:19.

168 Now I was living: See David Remnick's article "The Devil Problem," from the profile he wrote about these events and the research that came from them, in a book of his collected essays, *The Devil Problem and Other True Stories* (New York: Vintage, 1996).

169 In the original: *Mark* 15:14–17.

169 This version ends: Ibid., 16:8.

170 This second ending: Ibid., 16:9–20.

170 Then Luke adds: *Luke* 24:1–35.

170 Like Mark's second ending: Ibid., 24:36–53.

171 In Matthew's final scene: *Matthew* 28:1–20.

172 And how could hope: *Mark* 13:19.

173 Luke says that: *Luke* 10:18.

174 He says, for example: *Mark* 14:23-25.

174 Jesus declares: Ibid., 14:60-62.

175 I recalled lines: Wallace Stevens, "The Well Dressed Man with a Beard," first published in *Parts of a World* (1942), in: *Collected Poetry and Prose of Wallace Stevens*, eds. J. Richardson and F. Kermode (New York: Library of America, 1997), 224.

176 "Jesus says": *Gospel of Thomas* (NHC II,2), saying 3. Note that these, and others cited, are my translation.

177 Although we're often unaware: Ibid., saying 24.

178 Instead, as one saying: Ibid., saying 5.

178 The poem called *Thunder, Complete Mind*: While translators most often render the title of this poem as *Thunder, Perfect Mind*, I have translated the Greek term *telios* more accurately as "complete"—a mind capable of embracing paradox.

179 "I am the first": *Thunder, Complete Mind* (NHC V,2), 13:5-19:34.

180 One scholar, noting allusions: Bentley Layton, "The Riddle of the Thunder," *Nag Hammadi, Gnosticism, and Early Christianity*, ed. C. Hedrick (Peabody, MA: Hendrickson, 1986), 37-54.

181 Finding new courage: *Zostrianos* (NHC VIII), 1, 1:24-4:13.

181 Here a spiritual teacher: *Allogenes* (NHC XI,3), 52:15; 56:16-20.

182 Then, he says: Ibid., 52:9-12.

CHAPTER 8: LISTENING TO THUNDER

190 Another revelation: *The Secret Revelation of John* (NHC II,1), 2:9-14.

191 To simplify such questions: For an example of such denunciations, see Irenaeus, *Against Heresies*, V.26.

192 Writing his famous prescription: Tertullian, *Prescription Against Heretics*, 10.

192 When such Christians: Ibid., 13.

194 Long before that: For discussion of Augustine's view of "original sin," see Pagels, *Adam, Eve, and the Serpent*, chapter 5.

194 Evangelicals at Peninsula Bible Church: This phrase actually

comes from the author of the New Testament *Epistle to the Hebrews*, 9:22, when referring to ancient Israel's sacrificial practice (see *Leviticus* 17:1–15).

194 "God so loved the world": *Gospel of John* 3:16.

195 "Christ died for our sins": *1 Corinthians* 15:3–8.

195 Although he'd never met: *Galatians* 1:8–9.

196 Disagreeing, they'd split: *1 Corinthians* 1:12.

196 Determined to stop: Ibid., 3:1–2.

196 Instead, he says: Ibid., 2:1–2

196 For Paul says: Ibid., 1:21.

197 "We *do* teach wisdom": Ibid., 2:6–8.

197 Only those whom: Ibid., 2:9–13.

197 "the deep things of God": Ibid., 2:10.

197 "the mature": Ibid., 2:6.

197 "You're not that": Ibid., 2:2.

197 He begins with: *Gospel of Truth* (NHC I,3), 1:16–18.

198 "in the beginning": *Genesis* 1:1.

198 Often they looked: Ibid., 1:2.

198 "a wind (or spirit, *ruah*)": Ibid., 1:2.

198 "When he marked": *Proverbs* 8:22–31.

199 "I am the thought": *Thunder, Complete Mind* (NHC VI,2, VI,13–21,32); note that what's quoted here are only excerpts.

199 But certain rabbis: Perhaps most famously articulated, for example, in *Mishnah Hagigah* 2:1.

199 When Paul and his followers: See, for example, *1 Corinthians* 2:6; *Colossians* 1:10–17.

200 Overwhelmed by grief: *Gospel of Truth* (NHC I,3), 17:4–36.

200 When the Father sees: Ibid., 18:16; 24:1–9.

201 Thus the author suggests: Ibid., 18:24–31.

201 Instead of seeing suffering: *Colossians* 1:27.

201 "the mystery of Christ": Ibid., 1:27.

202 So rather than see: *Gospel of Truth* (NHC I,3), 19:34–35.

202 "O such great teaching!": *Gospel of Truth* (NHC I,3), 20:23–31.

202 But what we can know: *Acts* 18:28.

203 "So, the speaker concludes": *Gospel of Truth* (NHC I,3), 26:19–20.

203 Those who lack: Ibid., 28:16–29:25.

204 "Speak the truth": Ibid., 32:31–33:8.

205 James defines religion: William James, *The Varieties of Religious Experience* (New York: Penguin Classics, 1985), 35.

207 Suddenly revealing himself: *The Acts of Peter and the Twelve Apostles* (NHC VI,1), 11:18–26.

Index

Note: Page references in *italics* indicate photographs.